"A must-read for anyone looking to harness the power of data. *Be Data Analytical* stands out as a comprehensive guide that empowers readers to unlock the hidden potential within their data, driving innovation and growth in any field."
Bernard Marr, Founder and CEO, Bernard Marr & Co

"Jordan Morrow's passion and enthusiasm for data shines through. Breaking down analytics into four accessible levels means this book is for everyone. Its real-life examples and analogies bring to life the importance of understanding and implementing good analytics."
Susan Walsh, Founder and Managing Director, The Classification Guru

"This book provides an excellent framework for data-driven decision making in organizations. By framing the analytics implementations progressively through the four levels of analytics, *Be Data Analytical* is easy to follow as an analytics guidebook. At each stage, the book covers key definitions, roles of the different enterprise players, numerous business examples, and strategy suggestions to get the analytics job done."
Kirk Borne, Founder, Data Leadership Group

"*Be Data Analytical* is a book about leadership, decision making, staying ahead and having your own built-in systems. A consummate storyteller, Jordan Morrow speaks to those who know this space and those who perhaps need to. The data environment has changed forever and the complexity and challenge for leaders means the rule book we used to follow, and our previous frames of reference, are redundant. New ways of thinking and improving decision making are therefore vital."
Mike Roe, CEO, Tensense.AI

"Data analytics is a crucial aspect of decision making in the modern business landscape, and this book provides a comprehensive guide to understanding its nuances. The author's expertise and passion for the subject is present in every chapter, making this book a must-read for anyone seeking to improve their data literacy and enhance their decision-making skills. I highly recommend this book to anyone looking to unlock the power of data analytics in their organization."
Esther Munyi, Chief Data and Analytics Officer, Sasfin

Be Data Analytical

How to use analytics to turn data into value

Jordan Morrow

KoganPage

First published in Great Britain and the United States in 2023 by Kogan Page Limited

2nd Floor, 45 Gee Street
London
EC1V 3RS
United Kingdom

8 W 38th Street, Suite 902
New York, NY 10018
USA

4737/23 Ansari Road
Daryaganj
New Delhi 110002
India

www.koganpage.com

Kogan Page books are printed on paper from sustainable forests.

ISBNs
Hardback   978 1 3986 0930 3
Paperback   978 1 3986 0928 0
Ebook   978 1 3986 0929 7

British Library Cataloguing-in-Publication Data
A CIP record for this book is available from the British Library.

Library of Congress Cataloging-in-Publication Data
Names: Morrow, Jordan, author.
Title: Be data analytical : how to use analytics to turn data into value / Jordan Morrow.
Description: 1 Edition. | New York : Kogan Page Inc, [2023] | Includes bibliographical references and index.
Identifiers: LCCN 2023010366 (print) | LCCN 2023010367 (ebook) | ISBN 9781398609280 (paperback) | ISBN 9781398609303 (hardback) | ISBN 9781398609297 (ebook)
Subjects: LCSH: Organizational effectiveness. | Business–Data processing. | Decision making–Data processing. | Strategic planning. | Information resources management.
Classification: LCC HD58.9 .M6773 2023 (print) | LCC HD58.9 (ebook) | DDC 658.4/013–dc23/eng/20230410
LC record available at https://lccn.loc.gov/2023010366
LC ebook record available at https://lccn.loc.gov/2023010367

Typeset by Integra Software Services, Pondicherry
Print production managed by Jellyfish
Printed and bound by CPI Group (UK) Ltd, Croydon, CR0 4YY

To my beautiful wife and wonderful children. Without your support on my crazy data literacy journey, this book would not be here today. Thank you for all you do to support this big nerd.

CONTENTS

ABOUT THE AUTHOR

Jordan Morrow loves the world of data and analytics, previously publishing two books on the subject: *Be Data Literate* and *Be Data Driven*. Jordan is Vice President and Head of Data and Analytics at BrainStorm and has served as the Chair of the Advisory Board for the Data Literacy Project. He is an active voice in the data and analytics community. Jordan is the proud father of five wonderful children and husband to a beautiful, powerful, and successful wife. He is a fitness nut who loves to work out and has run multiple ultra-marathons. He loves a challenge and pushing himself. Although data and analytics are an absolute passion of his, time with his family comes first.

ACKNOWLEDGMENTS

To the many colleagues and friends who have supported my data and analytics career. I have many to thank and I would probably miss one or two if I just listed them all. I know a blanket statement may not feel as powerful, but to all who have helped me throughout my career, thank you. I hope you can all feel my gratitude for what you have done for me. A journey like I have had with data literacy and writing books is not one that would have been as successful on my own. What a journey it has been. I will keep riding it and hope for more success.

PREFACE

The world of data and analytics is here to stay, but did you know that there are four levels of analytics? Do you know your place within the world of data and analytics? Are you fearful that you will have to become technically sound and build yourself up to be an advanced data and analytics professional? This book will help the reader come to a better understanding of those levels of analytics. Take the time to understand where you fit within those levels and find ways to improve your knowledge. Along with this book, you can read the author's two other books: *Be Data Literate* and *Be Data Driven*. Although one does not have to read all three, together they help to build a powerful foundation of data and analytics for any reader. Jump in and learn today.

Introduction

In my first book, *Be Data Literate: The data literacy skills everyone needs to succeed*, I tackled the world of data literacy. In the book I looked at many topics, one of which is the premise of this book, but more on that in a bit. Data literacy is one of the most important and powerful tools in the field of data and analytics. My first book targeted more on the individual side of data and analytics, which when you think of data literacy and it being about learning, the individual makes sense, but data literacy can be a holistic thing for an organization.

My second book, *Be Data Driven: How organizations can harness the true power of data*, looks at, you guessed it, being data driven. This book focused on leading a data-driven organization, more aimed at leaders, but a powerful book for all in the world of data and analytics or who want to be a part of a data-driven organization.

This, my third book, *Be Data Analytical: How to use analytics to turn data into value*, focuses on the point mentioned in the paragraph above, a section within my first book. That section in the first book was on the four levels of analytics. In this book, I want to help illuminate the world of analytics. I won't be building formulas for you, I won't be teaching you how to code, but I will look to help you understand the four levels of analytics, how you can improve in those levels of analytics, and more.

Through these three books, you now have a series of learnings about data literacy, being data driven, and analytics. Let's begin here in the introduction to talk about the four levels of analytics through an analogy I use in speaking engagements.

A doctor's analogy

To begin, let's start by naming the four levels of analytics:

- Descriptive
- Diagnostic
- Predictive
- Prescriptive

There they are, the four levels of analytics. To help illuminate these four levels, I will be utilizing an analogy that I have used in my speaking engagements for, well, a while now. To start, this isn't going to sound fun, but you will understand it.

I want you to imagine you are sick. See, not so fun, right? Now, imagine you are sick and you call the doctor's office right away to make an appointment to be seen. The day arrives and you are sitting in the doctor's office when the doctor enters the room, looks at you, sees your symptoms, or hears or reads them, and tells you that you are sick. Maybe they even say it with enthusiasm. The doctor then leaves the room and never returns. Would you like to see this doctor again? I am going to assume the answer is no. You wouldn't benefit as much as you should be able to with a good doctor. This doctor was able to describe that you are sick, but that was it. Can you guess what this doctor did? This doctor did descriptive analytics, they described what was happening. Do you think this happens in the business world? The answer is absolutely, yes!

In the business world we see data visualizations often, we see numbers, we have dashboards, our favorite metrics, KPIs (key performance indicators), but guess where most businesses are stuck? In descriptive analytics! Businesses do lots of numbers and data, but just describing what is happening is just a description. We need to move beyond that. Just like we want a doctor to not just tell us we are sick, we want the doctor to tell us why we are sick. In business, we can see the graphs and charts, we can see numbers and compare them against other numbers, but this is not telling us why something is occurring. We need to do better.

Now, I want you to picture the doctor staying in the room and saying you are sick—here is why. That doctor has now diagnosed you. In business and analytics, it is the same thing. I don't want to just see some numbers, I want employees to own those numbers and be able to tell me why they look the way they do. I want them to diagnose why something is occurring. For example, if we have a line chart or something going in a certain direction, I can tell that the number is going up, but I want to know why it is going up. With an understanding of the why behind things, we can make decisions or get some possible solutions.

> A word of caution: do doctors always get our diagnoses right? No, and the same things can happen within data and analytics. But, back to our story.

With the description that we are sick and a diagnosis of why we are sick, we then want to use the information to make predictions. We are at the third level of analytics. We know why we are sick, the doctor can tell us what to do to get better. "If you do a, b, c, then x, y, z can occur." The same thing can happen in business. "We are seeing a, b, and c, so if we do d, e, and f, then g, h, and i can occur." The same caveat applies: just because we have a diagnosis, doesn't mean the prediction will be perfect, but we can operate and move ahead.

Finally, sometimes a doctor gives us a prescription to help us with our illness or malady. This is the fourth level of analytics. In this case, we can think of a prescriptive analytic as something external telling us what to do, like machine learning or artificial intelligence. We have an external something, like a medication when we are sick, helping to drive us forward with progress. Hence, a prescriptive analytic.

OK, I have simplified things down quite a bit here, but hopefully the holistic message is coming across. Throughout this book, we of course will be diving into these areas more deeply and effectively. If I didn't, then this would be a very short book. But please understand this holistic approach to analytics to understand the four levels; hopefully you can see how they work together more effectively now.

One note to make goes along with what I have said a couple times above: do doctors always get it right? Of course not and neither does data and analytics. Diagnosis is an iterative process, and when we don't get it right with medicine, we can go back to the drawing board and find something that works. In data and analytics, the same thing can occur. Data and analytics isn't perfect, it has flaws, but the key is to learn from those flaws or when it doesn't work and iterate.

Contents breakdown

Throughout the book, there are certain areas I want to attach to the four levels of analytics, namely:

- Data literacy
- Data driven
- MVP (minimum viable proficiency)

Throughout the book, you will find, I tie into each of these areas to help us build our understanding of the four levels of analytics and how they work. It is one thing to cover each level of analytics, but tying it to my previous two books and showing how these levels of analytics work through data literacy and through a data-driven organization is empowering and necessary. Let's go over each of these three areas real quick, giving you a foundation in the introduction that will hopefully help you throughout this book.

Data literacy

You may remember from my first book or be familiar with the definition of data literacy, but it is the ability to read, work with, analyze, and communicate with data. These four characteristics are necessary for organizations to possess holistically to be able to succeed with data. For individuals, they can have varying skills and degrees of abilities within each of these four characteristics, because we need to remember it is not one-size-fits-all when it comes to data literacy ability.

Individuals will have varying skills through the four levels of analytics that help them to utilize them in the ways necessary for themselves. Not everyone will be technical and proficient in predictive or prescriptive analytics, but they may have the need to communicate with those who are. This can allow the free flow of analytical work to permeate through an organization. Plus, it can make that individual more valuable in their career as they possess skills that will help them and possibly their organization succeed in our data- and digitally driven world.

Data driven

What does it mean to be data driven? Well, we seem to overcomplicate this in our lives. To be data driven is simple. It means to utilize data and analytics, in your individual or personal life, or for organizations as a whole, to help you make decisions. That's it, nothing earth shattering or overly complicated here.

With the four levels of analytics, we will tie in how they are applied as a part of being data driven.

MVP – minimum viable proficiency

In the business world, we may be used to seeing the term or abbreviation MVP to mean "minimum viable product," but we are going to be using it differently here. Full credit to my friend and brilliant data storyteller, Brent Dykes, who started using this term in May 2022, before me, in an article titled "Data Literacy and Data Storytelling: How do they fit together?"[1]

I love this term and while Brent was using it with data literacy, I will be tying it in to the four levels of analytics. What is the minimum viable proficiency an individual needs to have with the four levels of analytics? What is the minimum viable proficiency for an organization with each of the four levels of analytics? How does the MVP work with data literacy and being data driven?

One thing to note is that the MVP for an individual or organizationally will be different for the different roles within the organization. I will work to touch upon this for each level of analysis and different roles that play a part within that level. I will also touch upon this for data literacy and being data driven with regard to the four levels of analytics.

Summary

With my favorite analogy in hand, the doctor analogy, and with brief summaries on data literacy, data driven, and minimum viable proficiency (which we will usually just refer to as MVP in the book), we are ready to jump in. Are you ready? Buckle up and get ready for more nerdy learning and fun.

Note

1 Dykes, B (2022) Data Literacy and Data Storytelling: How do they fit together? *Effective Data Storytelling*, https://www.effectivedatastorytelling.com/post/data-literacy-and-data-storytelling-how-do-they-fit-together (archived at https://perma.cc/2X2N-FN9F)

PART ONE

Data and analytics

Since you are reading this book and possibly have read my two other books, I am guessing you have an understanding of what data and analytics is. If not, this section will set a foundation for you and will empower you with knowledge on those two topics. With that said, I won't spend an exorbitant amount of time defining them, although I will provide what you could call textbook definitions. Instead, I want to discuss data and analytics through what I will call a data and analytics "gold mine" or in this case, a data and analytics mine. To help us discuss this mine, let's jump into this vast world of data.

1

Defining data and analytics

What is the purpose of data? Is it some magical thing that will empower individuals and organizations with more success than they ever dreamed of? Well, that may be hyperbole, but the reality is, individuals and organizations can empower themselves greatly with data and analytical power. To help with that, let's take a look at the vast amount of data that exists in the world, and in this case, how much will exist. It can be pretty cool to think on just how much data exists in the world. The numbers that can be thrown out with the amount of data can be seen as somewhat unfathomable.

There are many fun ways to look at the data, but let's just jump in and look at the total amount. According to the Statista Research Department, it is predicted that by the year 2025 data creation around the globe will be more than 180 zettabytes.[1] Do you know how many bytes are in a zettabyte? Did you know that term even existed? Let me write that number out for you, and know, there are 21 zeroes in a zettabyte: 180,000,000,000,000,000, 000,000. That is a big number. Isn't that unreal? We are producing so much data. Keep in mind, not all the data is valuable or impactful for us, but for now, let us bask in the amount of data we are creating.

Another way to look at it comes from FirstSiteGuide, which summarizes it by saying that it would take us 181 million years to download all the data from the internet today.[2] That article was written or updated in January 2022. That is so much data—181 million years to do it. I don't know about you, but I have other things to do than worry about downloading all that data, plus, I won't live that long. For perspective, science says that some 180 million years ago is when Pangea broke up.[3] Why are we producing so much data? Why can we store so much?

The reality is, the digitization of the world is enabling more and more data to be produced. With all the data being produced and the availability of cheap data storage, why not store more and more? Now, this won't be a book or chapter on cloud storage technology, but it is easier to store data in our age today. With data and analytics, having more isn't necessarily what we want. Let me give you an example. I may love ice cream, but when one gets the biggest bowl of ice cream, eventually the ice cream will lose its utility (I had a professor use this analogy in my undergraduate program at university). The last bite doesn't taste as fantastic as the first bite. The same can be found with all the data we are producing and storing. First, having too much data can make it hard to clean, manage, and architect the data well. Second, it may be difficult to find the right data that you need to answer your questions. Third, it may cost the organization, not in cloud storage costs, but more in the potential and/or opportunity cost found in searching and utilizing too much data to answer questions.

With all this data, one can say, "so what?" One can say, "who cares?" One can even ask, "don't you think all of this data is over-hyped?" One may come across amazing stories of where data was used or is being used, but does data back up all the hype? The answer is yes, the hype is real and justified. Yes, we are producing and able to store vast amounts of data, but data just sits there. It takes work to bring it to life, to make it analyzable, to empower ourselves and our organizations. We need to clean, organize, engineer, architect, and establish processes. We need to do a lot with the data. One of the key things we need to do is bring the data to life. Data has inherent value and it takes work to get it ready for frontend work, but data without analytics is just data. Let me be clear, though, that analytics without good data could be a very bad thing.

Mountain mining example

To bring this to life, let me use an analogy. Valuable minerals reside within the earth. Mining is a process of extracting those minerals and achieving value with them. I want you to imagine you discover a mountain with gold and diamonds in it—pretty amazing. You hope to extract a lot of valuable minerals from it, but aren't sure of the exact value of the minerals found therein. No matter, you decide to invest in it, hoping to receive a strong return on your investment. What do you do next? Well, you decide to build a mine and a company to source this value. For this mine, you purchase the land you need, establish the right infrastructure, purchase the right tools and equipment, hire the right personnel, so you think, and build out the engineering processes for extracting the gold or valuable minerals you find. What is interesting about this, is the mine itself has a lot of real value and potential value. You could, in fact, say that the mine could be worth billions and billions of dollars, depending on how much gold or diamonds therein. But is knowing there is value tapping the full potential of the mine? No, of course not. You need a strategy, you need the right personnel, not just ones you think you should hire, you need processes, efficiencies, governance, and control. What you truly need is a strategic process and plan, where you are doing things effectively, efficiently, so you can obtain the value you seek. In essence you need to extract the gold and minerals, and then you need to sell or turn them into value. Not so simple, right? It may not be simple, but you need to do this effectively for a strong return on your investment.

One company that has utilized data to help it increase value is Netflix. I would venture that many streaming companies use data to streamline their services; in the case of Netflix, the company uses data to improve its organization and create a benefit for its customers.[4]

To further our mine analogy, once you have the engineering and infrastructure in place, you can go about extracting the value of the mine more and pulling out the diamonds or gold, thereby finding the value or "insight" (yes, I am tying it now to the data and analytics mine we are talking about) within the mine. The extraction of the mineral within is a process that can be simple, maybe sometimes a simple shovel is needed, or complex, where large machines or processes are needed to extract the value within the mine, but it is worth the time, cost, and energy to do so.

Finally, once you have purchased and established your mine, then put forth the effort to extract it to realize its value, you then need to have a purpose or decision made with the gold and diamonds in hand. Whether you are melting down the gold or selling the diamonds for jewelry, whatever it may be, you need to have a decision around what you will do with the extracted minerals.

As you probably have guessed, the mining analogy is a correlation to the data and analytics mine I want you to build within your own mind, to utilize in your personal life and in your job/career. This is also an analogy that ties to an organization's data strategy. Organizations are storing large amounts of data. There is gold or diamonds in that large amount of data, and analytics is the equipment you need to get it out. Let's go through what I mean.

Organizations have this ability to build out their own data "mines", in this case, large-scale data architectures, modeling, engineering, and so forth. Essentially establishing the foothold necessary for data and analytical success, the organization has accomplished the first step of its organizational data and analytics mine. The data foundation, the architecture, the modeling, the storage of data represent the building of the framework and ownership of the mine. Within your data mine, there is value. Data has value. You are storing up lots and lots of potential, but you need something to extract this value. Herein steps our world of analytics.

Analytics is defined by the Merriam-Webster dictionary as analysis... well, what does that mean?[5] Analysis is defined as looking deeply into something that may be complex in order to understand it and its separate parts.[6] In the same definition of analysis from Merriam-Webster it basically says we are looking at all the parts that make something up into its whole.[7] Within analysis, we are taking a look at the data and information—in some cases it might be a massive, holistic view of the data—and we are breaking it down into its parts. We are finding its components. That is an awesome and amazing way of looking at it. In this case, we are breaking down the land around the mine to find the gold and diamonds within.

The analytics, with the data, turns data and information into useful and meaningful features and helps us understand its nature. With data, we have a powerful tool to help us try to figure out the "why" behind things we are seeing in an organization, maybe through dashboards, data visualizations, or KPIs. Analytics has the power to take us from large sums of data to value. In the case of the mine, the extraction brought out the value of the massive amount of minerals. This value was in the form of the gold and diamonds.

We live in the world of signal and noise. Have you heard this term before? Signal and noise comes to us from radio usage. With radios, you turn the dial to move through the static "noise" to find the radio "signal." Nowadays, it is easier to listen to our music clearly, but this is how it was done. This analogy of turning your data dial to find the noise is powerful. In our case, let's think of analytics as the dial we are turning and we are finding our insight, the signal. The reality is, there is so much noise in the data, (i.e. parts that have no value) and our job is to find the signal. This is all our data, personal or organizational. This discussion of signal and noise goes right along with our mining analogy. Much like a gold mine, where one has to sift through the dirt to find the value. As an organization works to find the insight in the data, it is important to understand this analogy of the signal and the noise.

Data and analytical skills—data literacy

Within the world of data and analytics, there is a need for the right skills and abilities to exist within an organization. You aren't going to extract minerals from your mine without the right people and tools in place, and the same holds true for data and analytics. In the case of data and analytics, this is the world of data and literacy, which I wrote about in my first book, *Be Data Literate*. Data literacy should empower individuals with the right skills and abilities to bring data to life. Think back to the introduction of this book. There are actually four levels of analytics within the world today, but the majority of individuals will spend their time within the first two levels: descriptive and diagnostic. Think back to the analogy I shared about being sick. We know there are nuggets of wisdom and knowledge as it pertains to you getting better, what is wrong and why, and then things to do to aid your recovery. The diagnosis from the data is the signal, but guess what? There are many different things a doctor can pick from. Yes, some would be absurd with different illnesses, but hopefully through the data and information given, the signal is found and all that noise is washed away.

This is the same principle in data and analytical work. Individuals within an organization should possess the skills to decipher through all the noise and find the signal, which hopefully then turns into growth, return, and amazing decisions for a company. Let's turn to an example of data and analytics at work, using one of my favorite data visualizations ever: Napoleon's march on Moscow. See Figure 1.1.

Take a look at this image, attributed to civil engineer Charles Joseph Minard. This visualization shows what came from what at a time where this may have been lots of data. We can see at the left Napoleon marching towards Moscow, moving in a direction from left to right. As we see this move along, we can see that the lighter line gets thinner, where Napoleon's army gets thinner, and then the return trip in black shows this occurring even more. What a wonderful visualization, but does this show us why it occurred? No, not exactly. Herein we have found maybe some signal within the noise, but overall, more would need to be done.

Overall, we are setting up a powerful picture of data and analytics. Let's look at more examples of data and analytics, so that our minds are squarely placed on what each is, which will empower us in future chapters.

Data examples:

- The information we receive to let us know about the current economic situation.
- American Express is an organization that has a lot of data. Every time one swipes one of their credit cards, data is produced for American Express.

FIGURE 1.1 Napoleon's march on Moscow

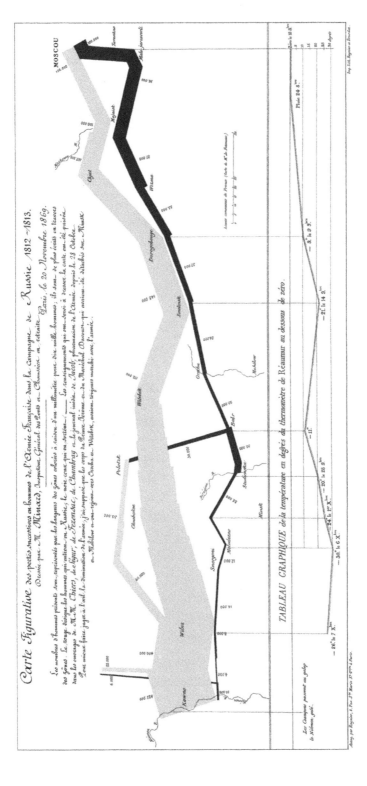

- Your birthday, personal identification number, credit score, possible information you provide to social media companies, and whatever else makes up personal information.
- The number of sales of cars by manufacturer.
- And many other forms of data.

Analytic examples:

- Finding there is seasonality within the trends of car sales.
- Insights provided by machine learning and artificial intelligence, usually in the form of predictive and prescriptive analytics.
- Retail sales forecasts.
- An organization's dashboards, usually in the form of descriptive analytics.
- And many, many other forms of analytics.

Data driven

It should go without saying that in order for an individual and/or an organization to be data driven, data and analytics must play a crucial role. To be data driven is for the organization to utilize data in its decision-making processes. It makes sense that in order for an organization to be data driven, data and analytics must be utilized as a vital part of the organization. OK, this might be a "duh" moment, but the reality is, the flow of data and analytics through an organization is done poorly in the world today. In some cases, very poorly. It is my experience from the continual invitations I receive from companies to speak on data literacy or other topics, that those companies are either investing more in their data literacy or they are not where they want to be from a data-driven perspective. One example of an organization investing heavily and in the right way is Miami Dade College, which is putting forth the effort to be data driven. This is not an organization that is data poor but one that is driving to be a "data-driven college" as the Madame President says. The school is investing heavily in the leadership dashboard and I had a great opportunity to go down and deliver a data workshop. What an example of doing things the right way. The Madame President is holding leaders accountable and she "gets it," meaning she understands the need to be data driven. With this good example, why are some doing poorly?

In the previous section, we spoke of data literacy. The lack of data literacy in the world today, it being the year 2022 as I write this, is staggering. In Qlik's study on data literacy, released in 2022, it was found that only 11 percent of people are fully confident in their data literacy abilities.[8] With such a low level of data literacy, is it any wonder that organizations are not succeeding in being data driven?

Another issue that we find in the lack of data-driven skills is the way data and analytics is dispersed throughout an organization. Does your organization have a holistic data strategy that is communicated out well throughout the organization? Do you know who owns what? Maybe more importantly, do you know "why" they own what they own?

Data and analytics should be dispersed and permeated throughout an organization. When we think of the analogy of data and analytics from a doctor's perspective, we can see the process or thought flow of you being sick and then a doctor helping you can work. In data and analytics, organizations can flow well like a good doctor, but it often doesn't work that way and is not as simple as me typing it out. This hampers how organizations succeed with data and analytics. I mention a holistic data strategy, but what does that mean with regard to the two areas of data and analytics?

With all the talk of data and analytics, it should be noted that these two things should fall within an organization's holistic data strategy. This idea or topic of a data strategy is one I will bring up multiple times in the book. I want to ensure we tie back the applicability of what you read in this book. Understanding how it is used, where, and why is important to me and is very important to anyone working, learning, etc., in data and analytics.

Now, what I mean by a holistic data strategy is a simple concept: a holistic data strategy is one where the data strategy ties back to the business strategy. I spoke in a Masterclass with Simon Asplen-Taylor and he described it as data helping an organization achieve business outcomes or objectives (I recommend his book, *Data and Analytics Strategy for Business: Unlock data assets and increase innovation with a results-driven data strategy*). Your personal data usage should be for achieving the goals you want to achieve. An organization's data usage should be to help the organization be successful in its field. I like the idea of "peripheral vision" within data and analytics. Peripheral vision within data is the ability to see "around" you in your data and analytical work, or "around" you in an organizational data strategy. In his great book, Simon has 10 questions early on to ask yourself or your organization. Here, let's ask some questions on peripheral data vision:

- Does your organization get tunnel vision in its data and analytical work?
- Are you siloed, just looking straight ahead?
- Or does your organization see all the sides, utilizing data and analytics, finding the patterns, trends, outliers?
- Does your organization buy tools and technology and empower individuals to succeed with both straight-ahead and peripheral data and analytical work?

These are obviously not all the questions you can ask yourself, but you should be asking these questions for your peripheral data strategy work—but also ask many, many others.

MVP—minimum viable proficiency

When we think of a minimum viable proficiency, the minimum skill set one would need in data and analytics, this could be a long, long conversation. We will cover this topic in more depth in the chapters on each of the four levels of analytics, but let's drive this concept in Chapter 1 with a further understanding of MVP within data literacy, being data driven, and what it may look like.

My friend Brent Dykes created an image showing the MVP of data literacy (used with his permission). See Figure 1.2.[9]

For this chapter on defining data and analytics, one can imagine that this empowerment of data literacy in an individual and in an organization is paramount to data-driven success. To have an entire workforce be able to do with data and analytics the things found within the highlighted portion of the picture can lead to greater data and analytics success.

When organizations look to fill roles with individuals skilled in data literacy, these are skills they should look for. When organizations look to upskill or reskill with data literacy within roles and employees in an organization, these are skills they should target. But what about those with more technical skills?

Each of the varying roles in an organization will possess a different MVP for data and analytics skills. Technical roles will require different MVP-level skills within the organization. I will touch upon different MVP-type skills in different roles when I cover the four levels of analytics. Please note that a chief data officer or chief data and analytics officer (CDO or CDAO, or other forms/iterations of that role) will have the purview over the strategy of hiring these roles. Also, the organization's data and analytics strategy, which ties to the business strategy, should spell out the roles needed and then the leadership hiring for these roles should own the desired skills necessary for these roles.

As for the minimum viable proficiency within data and analytics as it pertains to an organization being data driven, it goes without saying that if an organization does not have the sufficient minimum skills within data and analytics, backend and frontend analytics, the foundation of the data architecture, and the foundational skills of a data-driven culture, then it will likely not succeed in achieving its goals of being truly data driven. End of story. Without the MVP skills permeating throughout the organization, one may as well forget the idea of being successful with data and analytics. Sure, you may see pockets and bubbles of data and analytics success, even maybe a team or two that is doing very well with data and analytics, but the

FIGURE 1.2 Brent Dykes' image of MVP—minimum viable proficiency in data literacy

Key data skills to be data literate

	Read	Work with	Communicate
Insight	• Basic interpretation • Data skepticism	• Use insights to inform decisions and actions	• Data storytelling
Information	• Basic graphicacy • Basic statistics • Data curiosity	• Descriptive analysis • Diagnostic analysis • Data visualization (exploratory)	• Reports and presentations • Dashboards • Data visualization (explanatory)
Data	• Basic numeracy • Domain-specific data knowledge	• Basic tool know-how • Interact with, manipulate, and extract data	• Ad-hoc data requests • Data conversations

Data Literate MVP

holistic data strategy, the holistic desire to be data driven, has a higher likelihood of failing, and what c-suite executive or board member wants that?

Chapter summary

Data is something that absolutely permeates our lives and this trend looks like it will continue. Analytics is something that can bring data to life. Within data and analytics, always think back to how these things are a part of and crucial to data literacy, being data driven, and MVP. Think back to our mining example: data is in the mine and needs to be extracted. Analytics will help to extract the gold and diamonds in the mine. Use this analogy throughout to center your mind on the purpose of this book.

CHAPTER DEFINITIONS AND TAKEAWAYS

To end each chapter I will provide some definitions and takeaways. I enjoy taking notes as I read, and hopefully this will help you with your notes or may even replace them. Given this is the first chapter, this will be our first set:

- **Data:** Information that can come in multiple formats, such as numeric, qualitative, quantitative, even pictures. Data is just data and needs something to bring it to life.

- **Analytics:** A way to analyze data; it brings data to life. There are four levels of analytics: descriptive, diagnostic, predictive, and prescriptive.

- **Data literacy:** The ability to comfortably utilize data and analytics to help you in decision making. Data literacy is not one-size-fits-all but is the ability to utilize data where you are and how you need to.

- **Data driven:** The use of data to make smarter decisions. It is essentially the use of data to drive objectives, for either a business or individual.

- **Data strategy:** The strategy used by an organization to utilize data and analytics to meet the organization's goals and objectives. This can be for an individual too. For organizations, data strategy should tie to the business strategy.

- **Minimum viable proficiency (MVP):** This directly ties to data literacy. Think of this as the minimum level of proficiency individuals should have in data literacy. It can also be for an organization. You can also have minimum viable proficiency for each level of analytics.

Notes

1 Statista.com (2023) Amount of data created, consumed, and stored 2010–2025, https://www.statista.com/statistics/871513/worldwide-data-created/ (archived at https://perma.cc/B6TX-8ZGL)

2 Firstsiteguide.com (2022) Big data statistics from 2022: How much data is in the world? https://firstsiteguide.com/big-data-stats/ (archived at https://perma.cc/8Z3V-UYAD)

3 Britanica.com (nd) Pangea, https://www.britannica.com/place/Pangea (archived at https://perma.cc/KN4N-KZ4R)

4 Mohan-Finck, A (2018) How Netflix uses big data to improve customer experience, LinkedIn, https://www.linkedin.com/pulse/how-netflix-uses-big-data-improve-customer-experience-mohan-finck/ (archived at https://perma.cc/MRM7-8983)

5 Merriam-Webster Dictionary (nd) Definition of Analytics, https://www.merriam-webster.com/dictionary/analytics (archived at https://perma.cc/7HJU-T874)

6 Merriam-Webster Dictionary (nd) Definition of Analysis, https://www.merriam-webster.com/dictionary/analysis (archived at https://perma.cc/5MW4-SF5H)

7 Merriam-Webster Dictionary (nd) Definition of Analysis, https://www.merriam-webster.com/dictionary/analysis (archived at https://perma.cc/K6LV-SFWB)

8 Qlik (nd) Data literacy: The upskilling evolution, https://www.qlik.com/us/bi/data-literacy (archived at https://perma.cc/5LYX-NKPP)

9 Dykes, B (2022) Data literacy and data storytelling: How do they fit together? *Effective Data Storytelling*, https://www.effectivedatastorytelling.com/post/data-literacy-and-data-storytelling-how-do-they-fit-together (archived at https://perma.cc/TF26-YFW5)

2

Defining the four levels of analytics

In our introduction, we introduced you to the four levels of analytics through the analogy of going to a doctor. Each level of analytics is powerful, has impact, and needs to be a part of the process of taking data and information to insight. In Chapter 2, I want to define these types of analytics for you by utilizing examples from the real world. From these examples, I want you to think in your own life of examples of where you may utilize data in the same way to make decisions or glean new information. (Sorry, but if you think you don't use data to make predictions in your personal life, think again… what about that vacation you had planned and you checked the weather to know what clothing to bring? If you didn't check the weather, I am sorry and I hope your vacation wasn't ruined.)

Analytic level 1—descriptive

If we think back to our analogy from the beginning, the descriptive analytic was where the doctor tells you you are sick. The doctor is describing something, giving a description. Describing and description are pretty spot on for the term "descriptive analytic" aren't they?

The first example of a descriptive analytic I am going to make more general. How many of you in your organization work with dashboards of any kind? How many of you work with financial statements, like a profit and loss statement or a balance sheet? How many of you work with KPIs and see them quite often? Each one of these is a descriptive analytic.

These statements produce data and information that describe something, such as how the company is performing in a profit and loss statement or how we are doing against company metrics in a KPI dashboard. The descriptive analytic is doing a good job of showing us "what" happened, but it doesn't show us "why" it happened (of course, we will get to this in the second level of analytics).

Descriptive analytics is an absolutely crucial part of the data and analytics ecosystem that needs to make up an organization's data strategy and data-driven decision-making process, but I want to issue maybe a warning or caution: descriptive analytics is just a step and is not the be all and end all of data analytics. I fear that over the years, people have become so enamored with data visualization and tools like Tableau and Looker, that they think the beautiful data visualizations their employees make are the answer to everything... well, they are not! I wish I could say that more emphatically. A good data visualization is wonderful and powerful, but we MUST go beyond a data visualization to be successful with data-driven decision making. We have to get to the second level of analytics, the "why" behind what happened in the descriptive analytic. Before we do that, though, let me bring to light some other descriptive analytics to bring analytic level 1 home.

Fitness apps

I probably come back to fitness quite a bit when I speak or in my books because it is a big part of my life, but how many of you use a fitness tracker of some kind? Maybe it is an iWatch? A Garmin? Fitbit? There are many devices out there that can help us track metrics for our health. Sometimes, it may seem they track too much, or we may get too many data points, or, let's face it, *weird* data points that we don't know what to do with. I mean, with my watch, I get Resting Calories, Active Calories, Total Calories Burned, Calories Consumed (how a watch tells that, well... I don't know), Calories Net, Est. Sweat Loss, Fluid Consumed, Fluid Net. I mean, really, do I need all these descriptive analytics under just nutrition and hydration? Probably not! It can be cool to think on. When I ran the 2022 Speedgoat 50k, my watch estimated my sweat loss at 10,631 ml. Yep, that's over 23 pounds of sweat loss, as an estimate. That race was hard, I think dehydration may have played a part in it.

Overall, fitness apps can give many, many descriptive analytics and that is ok. It can be cool to see all these, but remember, there are underlying "whys" in them.

Social media statistics

Another area that is near and dear to me is the descriptive analytics that come to me on LinkedIn. I have been an active voice on LinkedIn for years now. Being known as the "Godfather of Data Literacy," I keep up on posts and sharing things on the site, with of course data literacy being a main topic for me. Of course, like probably a lot of social media influencers or other areas, data and information get back to me. It can be interesting to look at. Sometimes a post which you may not think will go viral, goes viral, and then you have posts that you think are good but do nothing much at all. Overall, you can receive these metrics and descriptive analytics, but again, I am seeing "what" has happened, but I am not knowing "why" it happened.

Baseball

OK, one of my favorite sports, if not my favorite sport, of all time is baseball. Baseball is such a fun sport and can be an amazing chess match between the teams, even players. Well, baseball is full of descriptive analytics. This was made famous by the book *Moneyball*, written by Michael Lewis and made into a movie with the amazing actor, Brad Pitt.

Baseball is full of metrics. Here are just a few to show you (some you may recognize, some may have you questioning "what the!?!?"): batting average, earned run average, slugging percentage, on-base plus slugging percentage, wins above replacement, weighted on-base average, weighted runs created plus, on-base plus slugging plus, batting average on balls in play… ok, you get the point.[1] Now, don't worry your minds over how to use these metrics, but know that metrics are used in baseball and sports to help in the decision-making process. It doesn't necessarily tell us "why" these numbers are the way they are, but it can get the story going.

Summary

Overall, descriptive analytics is powerful, as it helps us see what is happening and we can use it as a starting point within our data-driven decision-making process. A caution, though: don't see the descriptive analytic as the end game! Use it as a tool and piece of your data and analytics puzzle.

Analytic level 2—diagnostic

We have seen that diagnostic analytics is the "why" level. Think of the doctor analogy. You know you are sick and now you know why you are sick. To me, diagnostic is the most essential level of analytics. Why, you may ask? Because this level of analytics is where the rubber meets the road. Descriptive analytics is important, but it is just one of the early steps in the data and analytics roadmap. We can tell each other *what* is happening in the business or our personal lives, utilizing data to do so, but just knowing what is happening doesn't mean it will drive change. What is more important is knowing why it happened.

Gartner defines diagnostic analytics as finding the why behind the data.[2] That pretty much sums it up—we can move on, right? In the chapters on diagnostic analytics, we will dive deeper into what diagnostic analytics is, the jobs and roles that play a part in this important field (well, guess what, everyone has a role within diagnostic analytics, it is a big part of data literacy), and more. To help define diagnostic analytics here in this chapter, let's jump into my running and ultra-marathon racing.

Fitness apps

As of the writing of this book, I use a Garmin watch within my training. On that watch, as mentioned previously, it estimated my sweat loss during a race was over 23 lbs. I apologize, that is kind of gross to mention in a book, but all my watch or fitness app is showing me is what happened. Does it tell me why it happened? No, of course it isn't sitting here saying the sun beat down on me that day or humidity levels were at such a level (it does give me temperatures, but I didn't feel too hot, although it probably was warmer than I thought it was) or maybe I hadn't trained well enough. To find out the "why" to my possible dehydration or to my struggle during the race (I finished, if you are wondering), it takes more than just showing me some numbers. We have to dig in to do it.

Now, this can be a really fun thing to do, if you want it to be. Take a look at Gartner's definition again. It mentions techniques like drill-down, data discovery, data mining and correlations. OK, that is awesome, so how does that apply to my running? Well, how can we dig into the data and information on my running and on my racing? I trained often with my Garmin watch—what if I go backwards and look at my training leading up to the race? Should I go back one, two, three, four months? Can I see if I am improving in my training or not? Outside of my Garmin watch, what about diet? Did I record what I was eating and if not, can I think back in a general sense to how I ate? (Be careful here to not bring in a more "hopeful" picture of your diet because you don't remember well. Don't get caught up in biases or things that lead you to believe you did better in this area than you did.) What about the weather that specific day? I felt good during the race, I didn't feel it was too hot, but here in Utah, where I live, we had what I believe was a record number of days over 100 degrees Fahrenheit in the month of July. So, I may have felt the temperature wasn't too bad, but what if I just wasn't feeling it and it was warmer than I thought? Was the humidity worse than I thought? Finally, at least for this paragraph, I reached a point where I didn't want to eat anything, not a good sign during an ultra-marathon. That should have been a sign that I was dehydrated, or something was wrong, but why did it occur? Did I realize what was happening? Maybe I did, I don't recall at this point.

Look at all those wonderful questions that I came up with as I write this book. Questions are an amazing thing and a key/essential part of diagnostic analytics, maybe the most important part. We have the key question from Gartner's definition of "why did this happen?" but look at all the questions I came up with to know why I struggled in the race. Think about other things we could ask questions on for that race or for my training in general. We can then use the Gartner techniques to really drive it out.

One of those Gartner techniques is correlations. Think of correlations as relationships, things that *may* be related, things that *may* cause something. Now, we cannot get caught up in what may be the oldest adage in data and analytics: correlation does not mean causation. Remember that… please!! Correlation means things may be related. You may say that the heat was correlated with my sweat loss, therefore it was the driver. Well, maybe. It is a correlation, and maybe a strong one, but it doesn't necessarily mean that was the answer. We don't want to get caught in assumptions because we see a correlation. Now, that said, we can see those correlations and use them to make decisions, which is fine. We just want to make sure we do it correctly, that we know we are basing the decision on correlations and that we haven't proven causation. This may be most important or demonstrated in how we communicate out the decision.

Summary

Diagnostic analytics may be the most important level of analytics because it gets to the "why" of what is happening in an organization or with us in our personal lives. Can we always perfectly determine why something is happening? Of course not, but we can get good at finding patterns, correlations, making assumptions on things, and then rolling with decisions. We will explore diagnostic analytics much more deeply in later chapters.

Analytic level 3—predictive

Predictive analytics may be the easiest analytics level to define because predictions are something we are more familiar with. Kids may give us predictions or test things out with predictions in mind. As adults, we make predictions in the actions we do. Predictions are probably a normal, everyday occurrence. SAP defines predictive analytics as analytics that predict future outcomes.[3] There are many applications for predictive analytics—let's look at a few.

Fitness

Let us turn to the example I have been using with the levels of analytics, my ultra-running. When I take a look at the descriptive analytics that come through on my fitness app, through my watch or maybe my Peloton app or even on the equipment, I can get data and knowledge on *what* is happening. I can then use diagnostic analytics, use my human intuition and gut feel (but combine it with the data), to get an idea of *why* these things are happening. Now, I can go in and make adjustments and do things to build predictions on how to do better.

In the Speedgoat 50k, I really struggled on the climbing, at times going maybe 20–30 feet at a time up the climb and then needing to rest. Was it dehydration? Maybe, it probably played a part in how I was doing. With that in mind, I can then ask myself, "What can I do to make it so that doesn't happen in next year's race? What adjustments can I make to my pre-race hydration plan to help ensure, if that is possible, that I do not experience the same result? What can I do during the race to ensure I hydrate appropriately? Can I adjust my training in any way to get fitter to be ready for the race?" Here, I have devised questions that can have predictions to them.

To help with that, I can answer each question with a prediction:

- "What can I do to make it so that doesn't happen in next year's race?" To ensure I do not dehydrate in next year's race I can adequately check the weather, knowing what is *predicted* (even here we are utilizing predictive analytics) and planning accordingly. I can plan a strong hydration plan for during the race.

- "What adjustments can I make to my pre-race hydration plan to help ensure, if that is possible, that I do not experience the same result?" During the week, I can make sure to drink adequate fluids to help me hydrate pre-race well. I can look at supplements to take, make sure I have enough essential things, such as sodium, in my system.

- "What can I do during the race to ensure I hydrate appropriately?" I can set a plan in place that will empower me to drink enough fluids, with contingency plans in place for when I don't feel like drinking at all (trust me, you may get to a point where you don't want to fuel, and that is not a good state).

- "Can I adjust my training in any way to get fitter to be ready for the race?" How much did my fitness play into my result? I can work harder to be fitter and ready for the race.

All of these are questions that I could answer with a prediction or an action. I can hope for a better result. I can test these predictions out in training and see the results. Here, we can see the wonderful cycle that can occur: we take an initial descriptive analytic, we diagnose it or work to diagnose it, we then can build predictions around it and move forward with our work, test it and see how it is going. Then, the cycle continues.

Weather apps

I mentioned this in the previous fitness section, but the weather app is an example that has predictive analytics in it. I think weather predictions and weather people get a bad rap. I admit, I have been guilty of giving them a hard time. But then I read part of Nate Silver's book *The Signal and the Noise: Why so many predictions fail – but some don't* and my eyes were opened more to the great work that meteorologists do, and just how hard it is to predict the weather. But, in our everyday lives, we probably all have used the weather app to make decisions in our lives. This is a descriptive analytic given to us that is a prediction of what the weather is going to do. I am grateful for this.

One time I traveled to Finland at the end of November. Without using common sense or possibly using my weather app (it has been years, I don't remember if I flipped it open, but I sure hope I did), I may have not predicted very well just what the weather was going to be when I was there. Finland is not a tropical destination at the end of November. But, imagine if I hadn't made a prediction on what I needed to pack with me, and in my off time I only had shorts and t-shirts. I would have been in my hotel room most of the time.

Fantasy football

If you live in the United States, you may have heard of this very popular game, fantasy football. For those who haven't, you get to pick or draft a team of American football players for different positions and each week they can score points in the system designed for your league, and you go against people in your league.

Here, if you are playing this game, you may be more of a data nerd than you know. You may be sifting through descriptive analytics and statistics on your players, diagnosing why they did as well as they did, and making predictions on who to start in your league this week, based on who your players are playing against and maybe even making a prediction of who needs to start going against the team you are playing against. See, you may be a bigger data nerd than you think—and people are more data literate than they know.

Summary

Prediction is something we live with in our lives all the time. In data and analytics, I want you to think of prediction as something combined with descriptive and diagnostic analytics. We are probably making predictions each and every day, but now I want you to combine your predictions with descriptive and diagnostic analytics. I am not trying to turn you into a super nerd, but let's make you more powerful in your predictive work in your personal life and in your career.

Analytic level 4—prescriptive

George Lawton at TechTarget defined prescriptive analytics as the type of analytics for what should happen next.[4] Prescriptive analytics utilizes the power of technology to harness what an organization or individual should do next. Think of the areas of data and analytics that utilize machine learning and artificial intelligence. Prescriptive analytics is where the tools, technology, and data tell us what we should do next.

Fitness

If I were to use technology in my ultra-marathon running training and in my fitness goals, the prescriptive analytic would be the machine or technology telling me what I should do next. Within predictive analytics, I am utilizing the descriptive analytics, digging in and finding insight with diagnostic analytics, and then making predictions. Sometimes that may be a guess, sometimes it may be a very educated guess, but what if I could utilize simulations, computer models, things that have powerful computational abilities to help me? Now we are getting into the realm of prescriptive analytics.

Imagine you too are trying to hit certain goals and progress within your fitness world. You are using a fitness app, a watch, maybe Peloton, or whatever it may be to hit those goals. Now, imagine it doesn't just track things for you, it is making recommendations off what you are doing and/or trying to achieve. Imagine it is taking in your input, along with many others, running simulations and algorithms in the background, and then telling you what you should be doing. Your app is making calculations at a much faster rate than you or I are capable of, and then the recommendation comes. It takes what others are doing, maybe those who are in a similar boat as you, looking to achieve the same things or similar goals, and it is using that information to simulate for you specifically. Then, you receive the recommendation. You may be seeing the need for data literacy here. What if you can't read the result well or have no idea what it is doing? Are you going to trust that information being shared with you? Maybe, but maybe not. We don't need to do a long explanation of data literacy here but having a solid trust and understanding of the recommendation is key to utilizing it.

Summary

Prescriptive analytics is the robots taking over... sort of. Prescriptive analytics is the machines doing a lot of the work for us and then we are taking that work and making a decision. That's it, simple as that. Don't overcomplicate this. If you are a machine learning engineer or work with AI from a very technical space, sure, you need to know more than I am going to write in this book. For the vast majority of people, it is understanding what prescriptive analytics is and then being able to utilize the results to make a decision. Hopefully, that clears up prescriptive analytics a bit for you.

Chapter summary

I hope through this chapter you have a sounder understanding of the four levels of analytics. Let's be clear of the end goal, though. We don't just want cool insight from a diagnostic analytic. We don't want just an amazing data visualization from descriptive analytics. We don't just want a cool prediction of who we should start in our fantasy football league (we have to make the decision to start them, right?). And we don't want to just receive cool prescriptive analytics and then not make a decision with them.

The key end goal of data and analytics is empowered decision making. That's it. How comfortable are you with the four levels of analytics in making a decision? Are you comfortable? If not, this book will hopefully make you more so. Also, utilize the power of data literacy to help with your comfort. A word of caution, though: don't silo off the four levels of analytics. What do I mean by this?

Forrester defined prescriptive analytics in 2017 as an umbrella for analytics rather than one specific type of analytic.[5] I don't know if I necessarily agree with this fully, as I think there are many things that delineate them, but a point can be taken from this. The four levels of analytics work together. You can have predictive analytics shown in a data visualization, so a descriptive analytic. In the Forrester article, you can see that prescriptive analytics can drive diagnostic analytics and be used for all levels of analytics. Overall, the four levels of analytics work together and can be a part of each other.

For the purposes of this book, we will delineate the four levels of analytics. We will talk about techniques that work within the four levels. We will talk about skill sets and roles that are a part of the four levels. The book will drive things that individuals can do for each. Also, we will speak of the four levels of analytics as part of the holistic puzzle that organizations can put together to drive greater success with analytics. Having a sound understanding of each of the levels and your role with them can be paramount to your data literacy and analytic success.

CHAPTER DEFINITIONS AND TAKEAWAYS

- **Descriptive analytics:** This is the "what". What is happening, what happened, and what might happen. Think of this as observational analytics—you are observing something.

- **Diagnostic analytics:** Think of this as the "why" level of analytics. Why did something happen? Here, we are using analytics to find the why behind things.

- **Predictive analytics:** Think of this as what might happen. Here, we are utilizing analytics to make predictions. We want to progress through and utilize predictive analytics from the "what" and "why" levels, descriptive and diagnostic.

- **Prescriptive analytics:** This is the machines taking over. This is machine learning, artificial intelligence. Prescriptive analytics will be what machines tell us to do.

Notes

1 Harris, B (2018) A sabermetric primer: understanding advanced baseball metrics, *The Athletic*, https://theathletic.com/255898/2018/02/28/a-sabermetric-primer-understanding-advanced-baseball-metrics/ (archived at https://perma.cc/3VJM-RHC5)

2 Gartner (nd) Diagnostic Analytics, https://www.gartner.com/en/information-technology/glossary/diagnostic-analytics#:~:text=Diagnostic%20Analytics%20Diagnostic%20analytics%20is%20a%20form%20of,as%20drill-down%2C%20data%20discovery%2C%20data%20mining%20and%20correlations (archived at https://perma.cc/ZK8L-ALC4)

3 SAP (nd) What is predictive analytics? https://www.sap.com/insights/what-is-predictive-analytics.html (archived at https://perma.cc/U4WM-EX8Q)

4 Lawton, G (nd) Prescriptive analytics, *TechTarget*, https://www.techtarget.com/searchcio/definition/Prescriptive-analytics (archived at https://perma.cc/9WFU-CZAK)

5 Gualtieri, M (2017) What exactly the heck are prescriptive analytics? *Forrester*, https://www.forrester.com/blogs/17-02-20-what_exactly_the_heck_are_prescriptive_analytics/ (archived at https://perma.cc/T9D2-MJPD)

3

The power of analytics in decision making

If you and I were sitting in a room and I asked you, "What is the purpose of data and analytics?" what would be your response? This is a very important question. If one does not understand the purpose and objective of data and analytics, it is quite possible to go astray in data and analytical work. So, I ask you, what is the purpose of data and analytics? Is it to build pretty data visualizations? Is it to buy the latest tool and technology? I mean, data and analytics tools and technologies can be pretty amazing, right? Is it to have a strong data governance structure? Is it to have the best and strongest data architecture and engineering? All of these things can be good things, when done in the proper vein and strategy, but no, none of these are the purpose of data and analytics. The purpose of data and analytics is to empower us and help us in making decisions. That's it. So simple and to the point.

I fear that over the years, data and analytics, the purpose of it, is either lost on people, has been forgotten, or in many cases is unknown. The world of data and analytics is full of hype and buzz words. We can see terms like AI, big data, even one near and dear to me, data literacy, take on hype and buzzworthiness. What does this mean? Let's say it means that people get so caught up in the excitement and possibilities of it all, they get overly enthusiastic and these things are not used in the proper context or manner. Let me make it clear: AI, big data, data literacy, all of them are important, but they need to be

FIGURE 3.1 Data-driven decision-making train

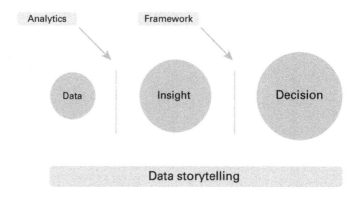

utilized properly and within a holistic data strategy. Each one of these can be a part of the process of making better decisions, but organizations and individuals just need to know strategically how to do it correctly (hint: herein is a powerful example of the need for a chief data and analytics officer... if your organization doesn't have one, work to help them get one).

To help us understand the decision-making framework with data, let's look at Figure 3.1. We will call this the data-driven decision-making train.

Here, we have the essence of a data-driven organization or individual. We will walk through each part of this in more detail, but starting at the left we have our data. The data is the starting point. We need good, clean, quality data. We need something to transform that data into insight. In comes analytics. From analytics, we can use a data-driven decision-making framework to arrive at a decision. Underpinning it all, we have the world of data storytelling to help communicate out the data, the insight, and the decision. This is a nice, smooth way to look at the process from start to finish. Let's look at each one of these in more detail.

Data

Data is just data. It has potential power resting within it. The back-end of data and analytics is very, very important. Without good data, how are we going to make good decisions? Within the data side of things we have the sources of data, data warehouses, data lakes, data engineers, technology, and whatever other areas that are along the backend of data. Now, there is so much data in the world today and that is going to increase, but let me ask, is it the amount of data or the right data that matters?

That may seem like an obvious answer, because of course it is the right data that matters. But, the reality is, one can get caught up in the enormity of data or the inexpensive cost to store data and forget that what really matters is how the data is helping us to meet our goals and objectives more effectively. That is the key. That is essential in an overall data-driven decision-making process. As you look to harness the power of data effectively, keep your compass focused on the goal of using the data to help you and/or your organization to reach your individual or organizational goals.

We don't need to do a long portion on the data itself. There are many books out there on data, data architecture, etc. Let's now focus on how to bring the data to life to realize its potential.

Analytics

The title of this chapter is "The power of analytics in decision making," so what is the purpose of analytics in decision making? Let's think about something with the potential harnessed and ready to go, something with power within it that needs something to ignite that power.

To use it as a story, let me speak of one of my favorite roller coasters. This roller coaster is one that starts flat on the ground. The magnets ignite and the coaster is propelled forward through the ride, now going up and down and around, even taking you upside down in a loop. As you wait in line or in the coaster car as it is taken to its starting point, and once at the starting point, you still have to wait; there is potential building up. You have anticipation of what's ahead, maybe some nerves or fears. Once those magnets turn on, that car is pulled forward quickly and you are off. Let's look at those magnets as the four levels of analytics.

Data is powerful. Using the right data, knowing your organizational business objectives and goals, and then utilizing and empowering that data to flow through to a decision can be amazing. Are there bumps in the road? Yes, of course, let's just hope no big bumps on a coaster. But, data is the anticipation, data is sitting there and it needs the magnets to bring it to life! In steps analytics, it lights the fire and gets the whole thing flowing. Let's speak on each level of analytics quickly and how it can help shape the decision-making process.

Descriptive analytics

Descriptive analytics is an essential part of the decision-making process. When we think of decision making, we need to establish what has happened or is happening. The descriptive analytic can set the tone for the data-driven decision we want or will make. If you think of the decision-making processes you have in your personal life, descriptions of what has occurred or the current situation probably are 1) a starting point or 2) a part of your decision. Let's use two examples: buying a car and choosing clothes for a vacation. First, buying a car.

Within my family, we were looking to get my wife a new vehicle. We have a big family, we have five children, so having a car that fits us all is tougher, it limits our choices. We had one that fit us all, but my wife wanted to have a new vehicle for the family, I think for the purposes of needing a bigger vehicle (maybe because the kids were getting bigger). My wife was looking at a suburban to be the next purchase. But, here we have a descriptive thing at play: the car we had was not sufficient in size for our family (the diagnostic side we can speak about in a moment, the "why" is because the family was getting bigger).

My wife is money conscious when it comes to a big purchase like this and the price tag of the suburban, another descriptive piece, did not get her excited. She was close to getting it, but instead settled on buying a van, which to her was not as sexy, but more economical for our family. This became more apparent when gas prices went super high in 2022 and we did not have to fill that suburban up with gas.

The second type of description I want to cover for a decision is choosing clothes for a vacation. What do you use to understand what type of clothes to use for a vacation? Well, maybe multiple things, but in this case I'm referring to a weather app. We can turn to a weather app to see the type of weather for a location we are going to visit. This weather app can show us the temperatures that are coming up, or if we are planning far in advance, it may be a website that shows us the typical temperature and weather of that area for the time that we are looking to visit. It may be that we are going to Alaska on a cruise—well, maybe we need jackets and hoodies, not just swimsuits and flip-flops. Maybe we are going to Africa on a safari and to deal with the heat we have to pack accordingly. We are using the app to help us decide, a decision, on what to do. The app or website utilizes descriptions or descriptive analytics and we can make a choice.

Now, these are examples of real-life scenarios for using descriptive analytics or like things to make a decision, but what about in business?

In your line of work, do you have goals that contain metrics or KPIs? Did you know you are looking at descriptive analytics in that case and how we are using the term? If you are looking at a KPI dashboard or something that is describing to you a past week or month, you are looking at descriptive analytics. These can set the tone for you in your role and in your job. These descriptive analytics are there telling you the beginning of the story. They are telling you the "what's" of what is going on. But, unfortunately, this is where many organizations really get stuck in our decision-making train. Organizations aren't doing that great at getting past descriptive analytics. Why do you think that is?

First, we are very reliant on our gut feel, intuition, and what we feel is the answer. Now, I want to make very, very clear: we do not want to get rid of the human element in the decision-making process. The human element, our gut feeling, our experience, are very important, but what we want to do is to combine the human element with the data element. Sometimes the data element will outweigh the human element, and sometimes the human element will outweigh the data element, but the working together of the two is what we want to accomplish with data literacy, a data-driven approach, and decision making. Second, sorry to organizations, but they aren't very good at moving beyond descriptive analytics. In fact, they might not even be very good at descriptive analytics. But, the reality is, it is a journey and organizations are on this journey and working toward being data driven.

With descriptive analytics in mind, let's talk about the second level of analytics within our data-driven decision-making train: diagnostic analytics.

Diagnostic analytics

When we are in the process of trying to make a data-driven decision, knowing what happened is important, but knowing *why* it happened may be the most important aspect of the four levels of analytics in helping us to make a well-informed, data-driven decision. Knowing *why* the line chart went up or down, why the descriptive analytic looks the way it does, those are so important to the work we are doing within our train. To me, the diagnostic analytic is the most important aspect of the four levels of analytics.

In our decision making, when we are using data and analytics to help us make a smarter, well-informed decision, just knowing what has happened is one thing. We know how the marketing campaign performed. We know what our attrition rate is with employees. We know how the business performed in a given quarter. All of these "whats" are important, aren't they? But, let's think about it and go a step beyond: knowing what happened is so important to our decision-making framework. In the end, the goal of our data and analytical work, at least in an organization, is to help the organization achieve its goals and objectives. Knowing what is good, knowing why is better. Let's take a look at a hypothetical example: renewal of a customer to your organization.

Imagine that you work in and are a part of a customer success organization; you are a customer success manager. In this role, you have your book of clients and one of them is coming up for renewal. You are to present to them a QBR (quarterly business review) and as you are gathering data around this client and building out your QBR, you notice an alarming trend: the customer's usage of your company's software is down, and not just what you may see with some fall-off or what is normal. We are talking down drastically. It happened in the middle month of the prior quarter and has continued. This is an alarming trend and based off your descriptive analytics, this would possibly indicate to you that the renewal of this customer is in jeopardy. What do you do here? Do you prepare your battlefront, figure out a discount you can give them? Do you create incentives for them? Find some swag in the building to send off? Maybe those are some of the things you do, but I hope you would first take a step back and say to yourself, "OK, this trend is alarming, but time to go find out why."

This "why" may save your renewal. It is time for you to dig in and do some diagnostic analytics. You have your descriptive analytics in front of you, it's time to figure some things out. Here are some potential questions you could ask yourself to help in the digging-in process:

- This data has a drastic drop; I wonder if any of my other clients have had a drop in their usage that mirrors what is happening here? Maybe if it is seen in other clients, it is not a client problem, but a data problem. If that is the case, you can work with the data backend team to clean up the data and help you get it sorted out.

- Was there something in the client's contract that would have caused this? Maybe the client was on a trial program or was receiving a nice discount and when it ran out, they pulled back.

- Was there something that happened with this client that made it so a drop should have occurred? Did they restructure or have layoffs that caused it? Did they have a company initiative that would have diverted employees' attention away from your software as this took place?

These are just a few questions and I am sure many more could be asked; maybe you even thought of some as you were reading. Each of those questions may give you more work to go through, but the up-front investment may pay off with big dividends in the end. What if you were to march off and create a big incentive based-thing, offering discounts, etc., all because you saw the drop, only to find out that the data on the backend had an issue and as soon as it was fixed, the data normalized and returned to pre-data issue figures? Maybe you spend too much time freaking out when in the end it was just a data problem. Or, what if the customer had an internal initiative going on that caused the workforce to go heads down, but had a plan to return to your software when the initiative was completed? A little digging in with the customer or knowing the customer better could have prevented a lot of work for you.

In your decision-making process, use the descriptive analytic to tell you what is happening and then use the diagnostic analytic to tell you why it is happening. Then, you can make predictions, our third level of analytics.

Predictive analytics

Predictive analytics is a key element to the decision-making process: if we do this, this could happen. That sounds like a decision, right? Or, it sounds like a decision we could make. Predictive analytics is a powerful part of the decision-making process. Unfortunately, I feel that companies are living well below the overall analytical power they could have in a predictive analytic because they may not do too well at descriptive analytics and they may really struggle with diagnostic analytics. In my work, I have seen many, if not all companies, struggle from an overall data-driven perspective. Why are they falling short? One key issue is data literacy. Without a strong data literacy permeating through the organization, they may not hit the end targets they are looking for. I do not know if I have found one company that is excelling in the first three levels of analytics. This is a hindrance to the overall data-driven decision-making process.

Imagine again that you are the customer success manager and you found out why there was a drastic drop in software usage: the company was running a large, internal initiative that was pulling people off of your software. This brings to you a sigh of relief, but it also gets your mind working as you learn the details: what could you do for the company to help them in this initiative? You start to dig into the data and information you have on the company, combining it with your organization's knowledge, software, and information, and you start to find something within the software that could help them in the initiative. You build out a data story to share with the organization and start talks with them, showing how you can help.

So, if you had just freaked out based on the descriptive analytic and assumed the organization was just not using the software or something erroneous, you may have made a bad prediction or assumption. Instead, you spent some time, a key element of analytical work, and got to the root of the problem, the diagnostic analytic. You then found a solution to help the customer out. Maybe this was an empowering thing for the partnership and really enhanced the relationship and the renewal will be a piece of cake.

Prescriptive analytics

Having a machine tell you what to do, does that sound like futuristic technology? Are you afraid the robots might take over or the terminator is going to come after you? Well, the reality is, machine learning and artificial intelligence are powerful and can help us out in our data-driven decision-making abilities. A machine has an ability to do many more calculations, rapidly, than we do. If I give you a complicated math problem, it may take you some time to calculate the answer, but what about a machine? It can probably do it much faster. Then, when you think of it in orders of magnitude, the machine can help us get through many computations, quickly. Think of the ability of machines to run simulations and help us in decision-making processes, like in the medical field. Machines can run simulations on new things that may have taken years to do in the past, but now you can run the simulations quickly. Tony Robbins talks about this in his book *Life Force*.

Having a machine be a part of your decision-making process can be a strong benefit. You can build or have built for you the descriptive analytics, you can figure out diagnostic analytics, you can build predictions, and you can have the assistance of the machine with you along the way. As was mentioned, prescriptive analytics really can span the first three levels, doing those things, but I delineate on purpose in this book.

Overall, prescriptive analytics can be a big boost to your decision-making process, but it needs to be a part of a holistic data strategy and the big picture.

Framework, decision, data storytelling

In his book *Turning Data Into Wisdom: How we can collaborate with data to change ourselves, our organizations, and even the world*, Kevin Hanegan lays out "a 6-phase, 12-step process to help those at all levels of an organization use their knowledge, skills, and experience to make data-informed decisions that can help transform their companies—and sometimes, even the world."[1] Organizations need frameworks or at least need to know how to take data to create insight into a decision. Organizations can utilize frameworks to make this happen. Kevin's process is one way to do this and I encourage organizations or individuals to study his or other decision-making frameworks, empowering themselves to know what to do and how to do it. We can't just build visualizations, find insight, and be stuck, not knowing how to make a decision. We need to make those decisions, or what are we doing this data work for?

Once you have a decision, you need to communicate it out, or if you are hoping to persuade others to make a decision, you need to have good storytelling capabilities. The field of data storytelling is large and has become bigger and more important. We need people who can communicate well the insights they have found; we need people who can persuade and objectively show what needs to be done. From Nugit we learn that data storytelling is the end of your analysis where you complete a story to communicate the narrative and information to a specific audience.[2] Another definition comes from Microsoft and tells us that data storytelling is the sharing of information and your analysis to convince your audience of something.[3] Now, I don't think it necessarily needs to be complex data and analytics, but the point here is the same.

Overall, data storytelling is a powerful way to get your message across, for all levels of analytics and in your decision-making process and communication. Utilize data storytelling to share your descriptive analytic, the diagnostic analytic, the why, and to share your predictions and what the machines told you. Use data storytelling to persuade your audience, to help them see the full picture, and to help you and everyone else to make a decision.

Chapter summary

Overall, the four levels of analytics are an important part of a data-driven decision-making process. One should utilize all four when needed, to build your narrative and tell your story. The power of data and analytics is important in a decision-making framework, but remember, it isn't the only part. Use the combination of the data and analytics element with the human element to make smarter, more data-driven decisions.

CHAPTER DEFINITIONS AND TAKEAWAYS

- **Data-driven decision making:** Conceptually, this is where data is helping us to make decisions and not where data is the only source that is making the decision. We don't want to get rid of the human element, no. What we want to do is drive decisions using data and analytics combined with the human element.

- **Decision-making train:** This is the train that shows data through to a decision. First, we start with the data. The data comes to life through analytics to find the insight. We then use a framework to turn that insight into a decision. Finally, we need something to help communicate out to the organization the decision and that is data storytelling. Each individual has a spot on this train, you just need to find out where you jump on.
- **Data storytelling:** Data storytelling is essentially the communication of data and analytics, simple as that.

Notes

1 Hanegan, K (2020) *Turning Data Into Wisdom*, https://kevinhanegan.com/ (archived at https://perma.cc/MU5R-TQ3Z)

2 Nugit (nd) What is data storytelling? https://www.nugit.co/what-is-data-storytelling/ (archived at https://perma.cc/FMH4-7YG9)

3 Microsoft (nd) What is data storytelling? https://powerbi.microsoft.com/en-us/data-storytelling/ (archived at https://perma.cc/J72S-EH89)

The four levels of analytics: define, empower, understand and learn

Here in Part Two, we are going to truly dig into the meat of this book and its purpose. We are going to dig into the four levels of analytics and teach you about them in more depth. We will dive into the different roles and jobs that play into these four levels. We will teach you techniques on how to get better within these four levels of analytics. We will show you examples, good and bad, of these four levels of analytics. Through this section, I hope you walk away with a better understanding of the four levels of analytics and learn ways you can personally improve in your data literacy journey, finding where you can contribute across the four levels of analytics.

4

Descriptive analytics

What are descriptive analytics?

We have defined descriptive analytics for you already. It is describing things, it is where we make an observation from the data. Let's use Figure 4.1 to understand the continuum that is the four levels of analytics, and as we do so, let's look back to our doctor analogy from the introduction.

If we were to extrapolate from this chart, we would start at the top—descriptive analytics is the beginning point for us. Why is that? Descriptive analytics is the visualization of data. First, let me ask: how many of you reading this would like to receive a massive data set in Excel and have me ask you to find me the patterns and insight where there are over 100,000 rows of data and over 50 columns, and you have to do it in the data set, no tools other than what you see in front of you can be used? If you said yes to that, more power to you, but the reality is we use descriptive analytics to simplify things for us. Let me start off by sharing some examples of descriptive analytics.

Delinquency and write-off rates

Earlier in my career, I had the opportunity to work for a large credit card company. One of the roles I took on was to do descriptive analytics on delinquency and write-off rates. At the time, this was not too long after the housing financial crisis that brought the US

FIGURE 4.1 The four levels of analytics

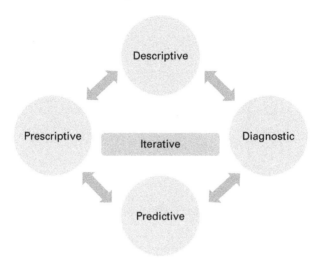

economy to its knees. In fact, you could maybe say the economy was still feeling the effects of the burst housing bubble.

In my role, I took a promotion and was given assignments to deliver reports to leaders and people within my company, not the least of which was the chief risk officer, a very intelligent and brilliant person... and yes, intimidating. One of the reports was a large PowerPoint presentation, which I believe was over 70 slides long, where most slides had at least one chart on them. Yes, that big. Firstly, I broke it down into six total charts that people could view on their phones. Each of us can take a step back and ask ourselves if things can be done better. I encourage you to do this with your work. Yep, down from 70-plus slides to six total charts they could view on their phones.

This report was an important one for the company as it was showing delinquency and write-off rates. In the end, I built the six total charts with a couple of the levels of analytics within them: descriptive and predictive. With that in mind, keep in your thoughts throughout this book how the four levels of analytics can work together, can be linked, and can show certain things. A descriptive analytic could be a predictive analytic, as you are describing the prediction moving forward. Plus, keep in mind just how cool these things are and how powerful they can be.

The six charts I built out were descriptive for the leaders of the company and should have empowered end users to see the trends through the end of the month. I will point out one key thing here that deals with data literacy and the 3 C's of data literacy: please don't just inherit your work and take it as is. Yes, it may be done in an effective and powerful way, but be creative (one of the 3 C's of data literacy) and see if there are other ways of doing it. I inherited that report and it was an Excel file linked to the PowerPoint file. If I accidentally delinked the Excel file from the PowerPoint file, yep, I was relinking it. I showed my senior vice president, still one of the greatest leaders I have ever worked for, and he saw what I had done and told me to send that to the leaders. Be creative. As adults, we get caught up in just taking what we have at face value and running with it. Don't do that. Think critically (another C of data literacy) and be curious (the final C), find new ways of doing things. I don't remember exactly how I felt, but I bet I felt great changing the deliverable from the large PowerPoint on down to the smaller subset of charts I created and then just sending those.

Monthly average users

Another area where companies, and specifically my role within descriptive analytics, are looking is software companies and people want to know the monthly average users. This metric can be defined in different ways depending on the company. What does a monthly average user mean? Do they have to spend a certain amount of time in the application to be considered an active user? This metric can be defined differently. This type of descriptive analytic can be shown and described in multiple ways. Do you just want to know the number? Are you visualizing it over time? Do you break it out by demographic data?

Now, one clear thing that I want to point out, and I bet this mistake happens more often than we know, is that descriptive analytics is just the beginning point. The question should be more around the behavior of the descriptive analytic and not just the descriptive analytic itself. If we see trends of descriptive analytics, the monthly average users, and don't ask "why" things are going the directions they are, what true value is being added? Descriptive analytics, I am afraid, is falling short of what it can provide for organizations. When using a descriptive analytic like this, make sure you truly know why you are looking for it or at it as a metric, not just showing numbers. Just because you have monthly average users going up, doesn't mean some initiative worked. Do not mistake correlation for causation, a familiar phrase you may have heard from statistics or data and analytics.

Weather

This is one I use a lot, but should be familiar to most, if not all, of us: the weather. We utilize weather apps or look at weather often. In fact, we can look outside at times and create descriptive analytics just by looking, although don't be deceived if it is sunny and just assume warmth. Where I live, it can be sunny and cold. But, the premise is the same here. You look at your phone and see descriptive analytics. Now, these descriptive analytics actually can have complex models behind them, but the nice thing is we as the receivers of that information don't need to have the complex model, just the output.

Within the complex models, you can have all four levels of analytics present and then you, yes you, who may not feel the most data literate, are data literate and can interpret the information given to you to make an informed decision about how to deal with the weather. I think that is something that should not be lost. We are all data literate, all of us, and we all have abilities to decipher data and information and use it for our benefit. We can even look all the way down to children and how they interpret information, and can then make decisions based on it. Children are a great example because of their natural curiosity (curiosity may be the most important thing in data and analytics, period). Use your data literacy skills within all four levels of analytics, marching forward and making decisions.

Sampling

Here is one you also probably see often and is a key to descriptive analytics: sampling. Sampling involves utilizing a representative sample and then using that information to extrapolate or project it on larger samples. One of the most famous ways we see this is in election polling. We see predictions on the candidates and who is predicted to win. With this, though, we need to utilize another skill from data literacy: skepticism. Polls aren't always correct, and we have examples of this. We should question things, absolutely, and make sure we are utilizing the information, studying and critically thinking on the poll, and then making well-informed decisions.

I will speak more to how we and organizations are using descriptive analytics in the next chapter, but now let's talk about roles that are involved within descriptive analytics.

Roles

In the world of data and analytics, the types of roles individuals can take on within an organization can be many. What is a data analyst? Is a business analyst the same as a data analyst? What is a data scientist? How do they differ from a data engineer? There is confusion around the roles, or maybe better said, a lack of understanding. This can cause problems of multiple types. One, if you are a hiring leader and you think you know, but maybe don't, and you hire someone for a specific role, what if it doesn't pan out the way you want? What if you aren't marching towards your goals in the way you had hoped? I feel that over the years, data scientists were hired with unrealistic expectations set upon them, and that is not fair to those in those roles. Another confusion could be for the person looking for the job. What if a job is posted one way and they thought they had the skills for it or had crowned themselves one title, but in reality they weren't ready for it? Finally, what if a person is looking to upskill and reskill themselves but the titles and delineations that exist are not clear? That could be hard for a person looking to improve in their skills but are confused, or don't know what the roles are and how they should approach them.

Overall, roles matter in the data and analytics world. Yes, there is some meshing of roles and overlap, but a clear distinction between them or what skills they could use, matters. That said, how do roles impact the world of descriptive analytics? Well, given that descriptive analytics is the first step in the analytical process, we could just make a blanket statement and say all roles are a part of the descriptive analytic world, but we aren't going to do that. I would be doing you, the reader, a disservice. Instead, let's go into some details on descriptive analytics and the roles that play a part here. Please note, this of course is not an exhaustive list, but it will take us to the right place.

Business or end user

OK, so maybe this is an all-encompassing role here, outside of the data professional roles themselves. What is an end or business user? These are the people using the products and pieces that are being built by the data professionals. In this case, they are those receiving the descriptive analytics and then using them in their roles. This could be a marketing analyst or manager, or even a senior vice president of marketing, who is receiving the latest dashboard on their latest campaign. It could be an accounting manager, looking at the balance sheet or income statements that were prepared. It could be the executive suite themselves, receiving the up-to-date KPIs, metrics, and OKR (objectives and key results) reporting. The reality is, a business or end user is a "non-data professional" receiving the information that is given to them. Does this mean that they aren't building descriptive analytics themselves or building data visualizations? No, of course not—let's explore.

The end user or business user may also have been given access to the data and information and given the opportunity to build their own visualizations and dashboards. The world of data and analytics has democratized the data, meaning this world has been democratized to end and business users. This puts the data and information in more hands, which in turn you hope can provide more and more insight and creativity, bringing the organization more insight and better decisions. Hopefully, those for whom the data has been democratized are also empowered in their data literacy learning so that the organization is truly getting value from the democratization of tools and technology.

Overall, the end or business user is a very important role within descriptive analytics and data and analytics in general. The majority of employees in a company will not be data and analytics professionals by title or trade, so they will be the end or business users. An example may help to illustrate this. Imagine you are an organization of 10,000 employees; how many will be data and analytics professionals? Maybe 500? Could it be less? Maybe more? The premise remains the same. If the organization has 500 of these roles, that means 9,500 of the 10,000 are not those professionals. They will be the vast majority of the users of the descriptive analytics. Ensure they have data literacy or confidence in their data literacy. To ensure confidence in data literacy, they can assess themselves and their skills and then plug the gaps through learning. Ensure they can use the data and have it democratized out with the appropriate tools and technology.

Data analyst

OK, the data analyst may be the most widespread data professional there is, but just what is a data analyst? Data analysts play a role to help solve the problems. They help build the dashboards and visualizations that the end users are using to drive decision making. The data analyst plays an absolutely key role in building out descriptive analytics. They are building the dashboards that show the trends and patterns, they are working to find the trends and patterns themselves. They are utilizing the descriptive analytics to then move on to the diagnostic analytics, which is the insight level of analytics and the level I find to be the most important.

Overall, the data analyst plays a crucial role within descriptive analytics, and data and analytics overall.

Data scientist

A data scientist is usually seen as the more advanced data practitioner and rightfully so. The data scientist is supposed to be doing the more complex things with data. By definition, a data scientist is one who uses the scientific method on data. So, if we are looking at the base level of analytics, what kind of role does a data scientist play?

If we are thinking about the advanced things a data scientist does, one critical thing is the communication of the insights they find in the advanced work they do, and this can boil down to properly building and communicating using descriptive analytics. How many of you would understand if a data scientist came to you and just started speaking in data and analytics jargon, using terms and vernacular that you don't understand? Would you maybe just stare at them blankly? Would your mind drift off to the latest episode of your favorite show you just watched? Or maybe, in my case, drift off to the food I want to be eating and/or a trail I want to be running?

The ability to communicate effectively is essential for the data scientist role. Communication is one of the most vital skills in data and analytics, and also in our careers in general. One way to do this better and better is the use of simplified descriptive analytics. Data scientists can use descriptive analytics to help drive and share things they have found. There isn't a need for a data scientist to build out and communicate through the advanced side of things. Instead, they should be looking to share insights and information utilizing descriptive analytics, bringing it back to the simple. It's funny how often it comes back to doing the simple things in data and analytics. Yes, data sets are massive, tools and technology are powerful, but in the end, the simple approach is a great way to get things across the finish line.

Overall, a data scientist should be using descriptive analytics in their work to help drive and bring to pass successful work within their given field.

Data engineer and data architect

One may ask the question: what does descriptive analytics have to do with a data engineer and a data architect, as they work on the backend of analytics? They are the ones who are building the data in the backend. The reality is, a data engineer and/or a data architect have a lot to do with descriptive analytics, and all four levels of analytics.

The roles of data engineer and data architect are designing the infrastructure of the data that will feed the frontend analytics. So, with these roles, it is essential to have them in place to ensure that the backend data is built in a proper manner that can be utilized to drive the frontend analytics. Don't underestimate the importance of this set of roles because they are in the backend. These roles are essential.

Leadership

What is the role of leadership and descriptive analytics? It is crucial within all aspects of analytics, as leadership will be asking for work that requires descriptive analytics. If you think about leadership in an organization, they will ask for things from a data and analytics perspective. As leadership is asking for dashboards, reporting, information on the KPIs that have been put in place, how the marketing campaign has done, and potentially many other questions, descriptive analytics can play a pivotal role in getting the answers that leadership needs.

Tools and technologies

The world of data and analytics is flooded with powerful tools and technologies... and I do mean flooded. I feel like new tools are creeping in all the time. There are many tools that are powerful and great to utilize for descriptive analytics—let me name a couple.

Microsoft Excel

I feel that Excel is looked down upon in the data and analytics space, but it also may be the most utilized data tool in the world. For descriptive analytics, you can use Excel to build simple tables of data, you can use it to build data visualization, or you can use its statistical capability. Don't underestimate its power for building descriptive analytics. With that in mind, please note, there are many tools that will visualize data in a more powerful manner (like Tableau and Qlik), but don't miss out on the opportunity to build quick descriptive analytics within Microsoft Excel.

Business intelligence tools

Business intelligence tools are some of the most powerful tools available for descriptive analytics. Tools such as Tableau have a big and dedicated following. Other tools like Microsoft PowerBI and Qlik are highly rated. Then there are others, like Alteryx and ThoughtSpot. These tools can be utilized to visualize and build descriptive analytics.

A word of caution I want to bring out here: data visualizations should not be seen as the end goal of data and analytics. I think that makes sense, but in a lot of cases, so much emphasis is placed on data visualizations, that the rest of data and analytics is forgotten. Let's remember that data visualizations are an important part of data and analytics, but they are not the end goal. The data visualization should be there to help end users get the insight they need to do their jobs better.

Chapter summary

Descriptive analytics is powerful and necessary in the world of data and analytics. We need to remember that this is the beginning of the analytical process and not where we should stop. It is good to understand what is happening, but if we stop there, we are not realizing our full analytical potential. In the next chapter, we will examine different organizations and industries so you can gain ideas for how you can utilize descriptive analytics more powerfully.

CHAPTER DEFINITIONS AND TAKEAWAYS

- **Roles:** There are many roles within data and analytics, which I will define below. Remember, you don't need to be the most advanced or technical person within data and analytics. Instead, find your skills and what you need to do within data literacy. Then, attack it and embrace data and analytics.

- **Data analyst:** Think of this as the first technical or professional level of data and analytics professional. Essentially a data analyst is one who may build or interpret data visualizations; they may possess some key skills in data and analytics, but may not be running advanced analysis.

- **Data scientist:** This is a more advanced professional in data and analytics. This may be one who is coding more, and running statistics with the data.

- **Engineer:** I kept this just as engineer. It could be "data engineer" or "machine learning engineer." Think of these individuals as engineering the data or analytics. They are more advanced in their data and analytics skills.

- **Leadership:** This may seem like an interesting role within data and analytics, but leadership plays a key role. This role may be investment or buy-in, but a leader needs to have data literacy skills and execute on the strategy.

- **Business user or end user:** A business or end user is one who uses the data and may not be technical. Instead, this is an area that is key for data literacy within an organization.

- **Descriptive analytics:** The first level of analytics that tells people what is happening. This may be found in data visualizations or dashboards, data stories, or reports. In fact, you may find descriptive analytics in various forms.

- **Business intelligence tools:** Think of business intelligence tools as tools like Microsoft Excel or a data visualization tool like Tableau—a tool that can help you build out descriptive analytics.

5

How are descriptive analytics used today?

Through this chapter, we will take a dive into seeing how descriptive analytics is used today. We will look more in depth at tools that empower this analytical level. We will jump in and look at the "democratization of data," which, yes, is a big word but is simple in concept, although difficult to implement well. Hopefully, through this chapter you will gain a better understanding of descriptive analytics and maybe it can help spark some ideas in your mind of how you, your team, and/or your organization can use this level of analytics even better. To start, let's jump in with that term: democratization of data.

Democratization of data

To democratize data means to give it to the masses, allowing people the ability to have data and use it in their roles. Hopefully, through the democratization of data, by giving it to the masses, we are getting more insight and having more eyes on the data, thereby giving us better data and analytical work. Unfortunately, as you can imagine, just giving the masses the data doesn't mean you are going to have more insight, more decisions, etc. That world of data literacy is necessary for the democratization of data to work well. Think about your organization—how many of your coworkers who have had data democratized to them are confident in their data literacy skills? How many are data and analytically trained professionals, ready to tackle the hard data and analytical work? The reality is, it is a nice sentiment, but you can't just give data to the masses and poof, magic happens—there is more to it. But, the reality is, democratizing the data should absolutely happen! We should be giving data to the masses and allowing people to dig into it, find insight, and make decisions. The democratization of data needs to come from the organization's data strategy. Leadership needs to own the strategy and the sharing of data, which can be part of the data strategy through data governance.

In the world of descriptive analytics, democratization is powerful and necessary. Let me share an example from my career through which we democratized data and put it into the hands of the masses. Oh, and another term you may hear with data democratization is self-service analytics. Self-service analytics is like it sounds—the individual self-serves within the data. You are the one building and driving analytics. Microsoft Excel is an example of a tool that one could use for self-service analytics.

In my career, I had the great opportunity to witness the democratization of data and building of self-service analytics. In our democratization of data, it was purely from a descriptive analytic perspective. In this role that I took on, my job was to help lead the building of the dashboards that we were using and train the end users on how to use them. I would travel to my company's headquarters to train and meet with people. As I remember it, part of that work was to learn and get feedback, allowing me and the team to build out the dashboards and make them more effective.

The big thing we did was to build and distribute from a descriptive analytics perspective. The end users were getting that first start and surface-level information that drove the business unit or those I was helping to have a good understanding of things from a descriptive analytics perspective. What it did not do was help on the diagnostic side. In fact, it was in this role that I started my data literacy journey, but I will share more on that story in the next group of chapters on diagnostic analytics.

This democratization of data is an essential part of a business's organizational data and analytics strategy, but we must remember it is just a part of it. The tools, such as Tableau or Qlik, are powerful ways to help democratize data and help bring descriptive analytics to the masses. The reason for this is that these tools simplify the data and can be learned by everyone. That is just the first step then. It might be asked: how can organizations, in an effective manner, democratize descriptive analytics? What steps can they take to help drive descriptive analytics to everyone? Let's drive some learning in this regard within each section of the book. One of the key things organizations can do within the four levels of analytics is democratize these levels out correctly. Remember, this is part of a holistic data and analytics strategy. This is not divided into the four levels equally across the organization. This necessitates a proper understanding of how to democratize this to the masses correctly. Let's jump into the democratization of data within descriptive analytics.

Democratization of descriptive analytics— tools and technology

The world of data and analytical tools is fun, cool, and powerful. But it can also be hard, have low adoption, can lead organizations down incorrect paths or can actually hinder the ability to be truly data driven. To begin, let's talk about tool selection.

What is it that should drive the selection of the tool? Is it the salesperson who can make the tool thrive and look amazing? Is it the latest and greatest technology? No, those things are potentially cool and fun, but the reality is they shouldn't be the driving factor. Unfortunately, they may have been part of the decision process in the past or a leading part of it—and still may be for some people and organizations today. What is it then? The driving force should be twofold: the skill set of your organization in utilizing data and analytics, and your organization's data strategy. Let's look at each.

Skill set

How can the skill set of your organization help drive the selection of the tool? Let's tie this to a sport I enjoy: golf. When you are starting out and learning, do you go out and buy the most expensive golf clubs possible? Do you think having the most expensive clubs will make you a better golfer? I hope not! It isn't the club but the golfer. That said, yes, better clubs can help. Instead of going out and buying the most expensive club right as you start, maybe you start with a starter set or ones that will work. As you progress, you get better clubs, a better putter. Also, the landscape you play on is not going to be the most difficult to start with. Imagine taking a first-time golfer to Pebble Beach or Augusta National and saying, "here you go, have a go at it." First, the courses may not like having someone who has never played before hacking at the grass. But, you may actually disincentivize the new golfer because you stuck them on an extremely difficult golf course. Instead, start them off on simple courses, maybe just the range for a bit. Plus, we will get them lessons to help them get started.

Within data and analytics, let's do the same thing. First, don't buy the most expensive thing on the market and say, "this will make you a better data and analytics person." You can teach a person how to use the tool, but it doesn't mean they know how to use data. Remember, when democratizing data, it is not one-size-fits-all. No, not in the least. Organizations can have multiple tools. But, when starting in data and analysis, tools such as Microsoft Excel, Google Sheets, and Tableau or Qlik are great to get going. Help the individual learn how to build descriptive analytics using tools that suit their skill set and needs. If a person hasn't really ever done data analysis of any kind, that is totally ok, let them jump in using Microsoft Excel or Google Sheets. If they haven't really done data visualization, you can also build within those tools or within Tableau or Qlik. The reality is, tools exist to get them started. Don't jump at giving an individual machine learning when they have never built a dashboard.

Second, just like we aren't going to have a beginning golfer start on the most technical and advanced courses, don't have a data newcomer or someone who isn't advanced in their data and analytics journey start within complex data science or engineering. Instead, help them by putting them in the right space to succeed with data analysis. Maybe it is exploratory analysis. Here is a powerful place to utilize descriptive analytics. If you want to get people going with the right tools and technology, have individuals who are newer deploy descriptive analytics. Have them build a dashboard or visualize data. Have them build a pivot table or analyze data, but have them build descriptive analytics to get going.

Now, as you have individuals on different parts of the data and analytics spectrum, where they have individualized skills and differing abilities, democratize the tools and technologies accordingly. We don't want to put simple tools in the hands of the advanced data and analytics professional and we don't want to put advanced tools in the hands of those who are in the beginning stages of data and analytics work. You can see how descriptive analytics can be utilized and empowered throughout an organization, but at varying levels. Herein also is where data literacy comes into play and individuals' abilities to be data fluent matter, as they can speak to and work through a holistic approach to data, throughout the organization.

Along with the skill sets that are possessed in your organization, another way to democratize data and analytic tools and technology is through an organization's data strategy.

Data strategy

Within organizations, the reality is that a data strategy should drive the work of data and analytics—yes, the four levels of analytics. When we think of the first level, descriptive analytics, the data strategy should help drive the tool selection that is utilized to help fulfill the descriptive analytic need and the needs of the data strategy altogether. Is this how it is always done?

I would like to give credit and the benefit of the doubt here to organizations and individuals. I think that many organizations have tried to utilize a strategy, albeit at times not in the correct manner, towards tools and technologies for descriptive analytics and data strategy as a whole. I feel at times we as individuals and organizations are enamored by the latest trends, by the shiny object that is presented in front of us. Trust me, those shiny objects can look absolutely amazing. When a descriptive analytics tool is placed in front of us and it looks amazing and it is run well, a beautiful visualization is presented, the data is captured easily and effectively, and we want that to occur with our data and the needs we have. The problem is, it doesn't work that way or that seamlessly. Instead, when we try to deploy the tool effectively on our side, we run into snags and other issues. This is how it works. That said, using our data strategy to effectively pick the tools we will use to capture descriptive analytics and the four levels of analytics as a whole can be an effective way to successfully deploy the tool. Yes, we will have bumps and bruises along the way, that is probably an inevitable destiny at times with data and analytics, but we can use the strategy to more effectively select the tool. The reason the strategy helps is it allows us to know if we need a visualization tool, a tool to help with coding, or an advanced tool for machine learning or other advanced data and analytics.

With descriptive analytics, we need an effective tool that the masses can utilize to help us achieve our data strategy, which is there to help us achieve our business or organizational strategy. So, if you are in charge of picking a tool to help you achieve descriptive analytics, take adequate time to achieve your goal of picking the right tool. Don't get caught in analysis paralysis, where we are just stuck looking at tools time and time again. There are a lot of data and analytics tools out there, and there are lots of descriptive analytics tools, like a data visualization tool such as Tableau or Qlik. We can spend too much time looking at them. Instead, dig into the tools and the companies, ask deep questions on their ability to help the masses drive descriptive analytics. Then, when you feel comfortable you have found the right tool that will meet your organization's data strategy, march forward with it. Provide the right training and access to the tool. Help the organization achieve the right success within the tool and technology you have purchased, hitting the first level of analytics.

Descriptive analytics— data visualization

One of the most common ways descriptive analytics is presented to us in the world today is through data visualization. Tableau defines data visualization as the visualization of data elements into different charts and graphs, and it simplifies it for non-advanced users.[1]

Essentially, data visualization is a way to visualize the data. OK, we can move on now, it's that simple. In reality, data visualization is a simple way for us to visualize descriptive analytics and data in general. Would you like to be asked to sift through a data table that has 100,000 rows of data and 20 columns? No? Why not? Can you imagine if that was your job? That would be a very hard way to drive analytical work. In reality, it is not efficient or effective. Instead, we want to utilize tools and methods of driving descriptive analytics in a way that can be easily consumed by the masses. Herein lies the power of data visualization. In reality, descriptive analytics are utilized and built powerfully with data visualization.

Dashboards

One of the key ways a data visualization is utilized to derive and share descriptive analytics is through dashboards. Dashboards are visualizations of data, using different charts and screens or space to show the chart, tell a story, and/or convey different key performance indicators and/or metrics. How often do you see dashboards in an organization or in life? How often do you see a visualization shared with you to convey a message? Think of the news itself. It may not be an extensive dashboard with many visualizations in it, but maybe we can call one chart a simplified dashboard utilized to share with us some sort of news or information.

How many dashboards do you see on a daily basis? For me, with my ultra-running and working out, I see a dashboard right within my phone app. Within your career, think how many dashboards and data visualizations you are seeing. Each of these contains descriptive analytics. What a powerful way for an organization to organize and concretely utilize descriptive analytics for its intended purposes.

One-off data visualizations

What do I mean by "one-off data visualizations"? Think about the pandemic with me for a minute. We weren't seeing or utilizing massive dashboards each and every day. Instead, we may have been hit by a visualization of something to do with Covid-19. One-off data visualizations are an effective way to convey a message quickly and succinctly. This is something you personally and your organization should effectively do. Here are some examples of one-off data visualizations that you may utilize in your career:

- **Current sales by rep with respect to target goals for each rep.** Now, organizations probably have more robust dashboards when it comes to sales, but what if you just want a quick take on your sales team and where they are in the given time period you are measuring? A one-off descriptive analytical data visualization is a powerful way for a sales leader to quickly see how their team is doing.

- **Current marketing campaign click-throughs.** Do you work in a marketing organization? Do you like robust reporting on the campaigns? Well, if you don't, I hope you will. Instead, what if you are looking at click-through rates and want to run a short social media campaign to see if you can get a quick bump? Do you need a vast dashboard or would a quick visual be strong? In this case, a quick visualization of some kind may be all that is necessary.

- **Pandemic-type scenarios.** This goes without saying, but the daily visuals we see can be powerful to provide us with quick information.

With one-off data visualizations, we need to ensure that if we are the one building them, we are building them with objective viewpoints. We can say that one-off visualizations are powerful and effective in their use, but we have to also understand that at times, they are misused and not done from an objective perspective.

Data storytelling

Data storytelling is a very popular and large aspect of the data and analytics space, with books written on it. I will not do a full book on it here, but I will say that data storytelling touches upon all four levels of analytics. Let me give my definition of data storytelling and then expand on how it plays a part within descriptive analytics. Data storytelling is an effective way to communicate with data through the use of visualizations and analytics, and helps drive forward the insight derived. It is also an effective way of bringing to life the data and analysis, tying it to organizational goals and objectives. Now, how does it deal with descriptive analytics?

Descriptive analytics is the foundation and beginning of a data story. In our case, think of a data story as a what, a why, and maybe sharing the how. In our case, the descriptive analytic needs to be the data visualization or descriptive data that shows what is happening. Utilize the descriptive analytic as a way to show the person reading the data story as the how.

Businesses are looking at data storytelling more and more, but I want to expand on it and not just say data storytelling. I think businesses are looking at communicating within the data and analytics profession as a key tenet and something that needs to be done effectively.

Industry examples

To end this chapter on how descriptive analytics is used today, I want to share some examples that can maybe spark some ideas in your mind on how you could be doing it differently. I will also end with a caution in the chapter summary.

Healthcare

Healthcare is an industry that is flooded with data and information. Think about how every time you go to see a doctor, more information, data, is recorded. How does the healthcare industry use descriptive analytics? Well, one example is a dashboard at a hospital showing how many beds the hospital has and how many are occupied. Pretty straightforward, but I bet this is important with regard to the healthcare industry.

Another area where descriptive analytics is utilized within the healthcare industry is watching the trends of an illness as it permeates within a given region. Think about all the descriptive analytics reporting that was done in your area specifically on how different regions were at different levels of Covid-19. I find this is a powerful way the healthcare industry uses descriptive analytics to understand what is happening with an illness in an area, but again, it is the "what." In the next chapter, we will expand on this industry example and talk about the "why."

Retail

Retail industries, like clothing or big box stores, can utilize descriptive analytics in different ways. Think of some of the bigger retail chains and stores like a Target or a Walmart. It makes sense that these stores would utilize descriptive analytics to understand inventory and when to supply or stock up again. If they aren't, I know of a job that someone needs to take on in these companies.

Another way that retail businesses can use descriptive analytics is actually from an employee perspective. If we are talking retail businesses that have actual stores, a record of busy times of year or busy seasons, coupled with the number of employees a business has and the hours that they are working, is a good way to know when to hire more employees or when they don't need as many. I have a family member who works more around the holiday time and I don't think they work at other times of the year, unless they are called upon. In this case, using descriptive analytics can show that sales go up around certain times of year and that an organization may need more employees on hand to be successful.

Marketing

We spoke about this earlier, but marketing can use descriptive analytics to show what is happening or what did happen in a marketing campaign. Descriptive analytics can be a powerful way to understand the demographics of your customer base and can be used to understand who isn't in your customer base. Remember, though, that you cannot use the descriptive analytics to then build campaigns that would be discriminatory.

Finance, financial services, and banking

I can tell you from personal experience that descriptive analytics is used regularly within financial services, and heavily. In my work I have helped to build descriptive analytics for write-off rates and delinquencies. This was important to know as when I was working for a financial services organization it was during the housing financial crisis. We needed to know the delinquency and write-off rates for informational purposes and for the various reasons different leaders would use the metrics.

Another way these industries can use descriptive analytics is through the understanding of products and what is popular and what is not. For example, if you didn't have descriptive analytics on the products you offer as a bank or financial institution, how would you know if you should stop selling these products or not? Please do not say we would go off our gut feel or what we see, because our eyes can be deceiving. Remember, we don't want to get rid of gut feel or the human element, but let's combine it with the data.

Supply chain and logistics

Having descriptive analytics to understand the logistics and supply chain of your organization or of the global economy is very important. Now, does having descriptive analytics mean we won't have supply chain issues? No, it doesn't, but hopefully it will help to mitigate them or provide a picture of what is happening. Hopefully then we can resolve those issues.

Conclusion

Overall, there are many different examples of descriptive analytics. In the next chapter, we will go into the "why" of the examples I have shared and maybe share other examples.

Data ethics and descriptive analytics

How does the ethical use of data fall into descriptive analytics? When we are building our data stories and visualizations, we need to ensure our objectivity to the data. Do not go out and look to design your data visualizations and stories to fit your narrative or what you want to see within the data. This is your personal bias coming into play and that should not be a part of the data visualizations you are building. Instead, build objective stories, objective "whats" from the data. This objective use of the data is the most effective way to build data visualizations and data stories.

Chapter summary

Descriptive analytics is prevalent in the world today. There are many examples—just receiving a metric can be a descriptive analytic—but remember, it may just be the first step. Now, a word of caution. There is a law in statistics called Goodhart's law that states that when a measure becomes a target, it ceases to be a good measure. So, as you build descriptive analytics, make sure that you are not turning those measurements into targets. Don't let a new target, that was a measure, misguide you on how to do things because you saw it in a descriptive analytic. Now, onto how to get better at descriptive analytics.

CHAPTER DEFINITIONS AND TAKEAWAYS

- **Democratization of data:** This is the giving of data to everyone. Granted, we don't just freely give data to everyone, but this is where an organization will democratize the access of data and share it out. Hopefully, organizations will find that more people looking at the data, under a good data governance program, will provide more insight into the data.

- **Data governance:** I just mentioned data governance above, so I'd better define it. Simply put, this is the program that governs the data of an organization. Think of it as who can have access to what.

- **Descriptive analytics: the problem:** Within the world of data and analytics today, this level, descriptive analytics, is where organizations can be stuck within the four levels of analytics. This is the easier level and without a good strategy and strong data literacy, organizations may not move beyond this point.

Note

1 Tableau (nd) What is data visualization? Definition, examples, and learning resources, https://www.tableau.com/learn/articles/data-visualization (archived at https://perma.cc/494R-AF3G)

6

How individuals and organizations can improve in descriptive analytics

Now, we get to the "how to improve" chapter. Here, you may think you will get tips and tricks to improve data visualization or some other aspect of descriptive analytics. Well, you would be right, but we are going to go beyond that. There is something that I have dubbed the "tridata" that will become a part of each of the "how to" chapters. If you were or are a fan of the video game series Zelda, which I am, there is the triforce.[1] In my world, there is the tridata. The tridata is made up of data-driven problem solving, decision making, and execution. See Figure 6.1 (and if you know me, I like mountains, so it is cool it looks like mountains).

If I were to just give tips and tricks, I would be doing you a disservice. Helping you to understand how descriptive analytics is a part of an organization being data driven is what is needed. Plus this will empower you to be more data literate, as it helps you to understand how descriptive analytics fits into the organization. Having a sound understanding of how it works in an organization empowers your data literacy; it isn't just a bunch of charts at that point. If I am being more holistic and helping you with multiple aspects, then I am being successful with this book.

A quick description of the tridata will be helpful before I jump into more detailed areas of improvement within descriptive analytics. In being data driven, there is a need to make sure that all aspects of the data and analytics train are covered. As part of that train, there are

FIGURE 6.1 The tridata

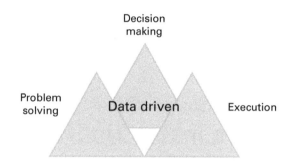

key elements such as the data itself, the insight, analytics. Here, we can see the tridata encompasses three main parts:

- **Problem solving:** How do we get better at problem solving with data? How do descriptive, diagnostic, predictive, and prescriptive analytics empower us to be better at problem solving with data?

- **Decision making:** How do we get better at making decisions with data and how does descriptive analytics play a part in the decisions themselves (think of the beginning phases and think of storytelling)?

- **Finally, execution:** How do we get better at executing the decisions with data? How does descriptive analytics play a part?

Another area we want to make sure we cover in this chapter is the MVP of descriptive analytics. What would be key elements of minimum viable proficiency within descriptive analytics? We will ensure that you, the reader, walk away with a good understanding of the key skills I say are necessary within descriptive analytics. Now, remember, I am not writing this analytics book in the same manner of other analytics books. You can buy books on data visualization, statistics, and other areas within data and analytics. They will show you great things. I am writing this from the perspective of being more data driven. Of how you can apply descriptive analytics to the tridata seen in Figure 6.1. I am helping the reader get a good grasp of where they sit within the data and analytics train and how they can execute in a more intelligent way within data-driven processes. Let's jump into the tridata to start. As you will see, I will tie in "usual" ways of looking at analytics, like data visualization, throughout the process of going through the tridata and MVP.

Descriptive analytics and data-driven problem solving

The first area of the tridata I want to discuss within the world of descriptive analytics is problem solving. We know that we need data, we know we need backend data to be trustworthy (think of the world of data management here—there are plenty of books you can grab to study this and what it is), and we need the key pieces of data to drive to a decision. In our case, we are looking at the first step of the tridata to be problem solving.

Problem solving is like it says, we are solving a problem. Within the space of data and analytics, what kind of problem are we solving? Well, I hope you answered this to be a business problem. Descriptive analytics can help us understand what is happening with a marketing campaign—this is a business question we are looking to have answered. The end goal of descriptive analytics and data is not a cool visualization or idea, but a cool visualization or idea that ties back to a business objective. When I say problem solving, it may be a problem we are solving but is more. It is that we are also solving and executing towards our business goals and objectives. In this case, we can think of problem solving as a "how to" get to where we want to be. How does descriptive analytics do this and how do we get better at using descriptive analytics in our problem solving?

First, think of descriptive analytics as the starting point of analytics and problem solving. To problem-solve or solve for a key objective for our team, business unit, or company, involves helping us to understand the problem or objective we are solving. Descriptive analytics should absolutely be a key element to understanding the situation. Context matters so much. How can we gain greater context than just our hunches or gut feel? We can turn to descriptive analytics. A big note here, though: I don't want you to think we are getting rid of gut feel and hunches. No, we like those. Each of you has experience, ideas, and thoughts; just make sure you combine that with the data. Sometimes, your thoughts and ideas will need to outweigh the data and sometimes the data will need to outweigh the thoughts, but that's ok. We want to seek harmony between the data and the human element over the long haul. So, don't fret, your personal thoughts and ideas are important in the world of data and analytics. Also, this shows that everyone has a seat at the data and analytics table. You may not have the technical skills of others, but you have your own ideas and thoughts. Bring those to the table, work as a team, and drive to the best outcome.

So, with descriptive analytics as the starting point, how do we improve upon it? The first step might seem a bit off or weird, but trust me, this is a vital step in the data and analytics train and moving towards being more data driven. The first step is improving our mindset.

Mindset improvement

Why would I say that mindset improvement is step number one? Well, data and analytics requires a data- and analytically driven mindset. This means truly understanding the data and analytics train, and understanding how to be objective versus bringing our own biases to the table. It means being willing to question data and the data others present (granted, you need to communicate well to do this and know how to question others effectively), and it means being willing to have your own ideas and data challenged. Mindset matters greatly. Data literacy and being data driven are not just about the data and technology. On the contrary, mindset and dealing with people probably matter more. So, take a minute to answer these questions personally to determine where your data and analytical mindset is:

- When I receive data, do I just take it at face value or do I take time to question it and think on it?
- When I build data and analytics, do I get offended when someone critiques or questions what I have built?

- When I run a data and analytics project, do I get upset when things don't turn out the way I want or do I attack it from an iterative approach?
- Do I laugh or think someone's question is silly when they bring it to me?
- Do I rely only on those who are data and analytics professionals or do I bring others to the table?

Seriously evaluate these questions with an open mind. Don't hinder your data-driven work because you don't want to answer these questions honestly. If you want to improve within descriptive and all four levels of analytics, your mindset has to be right and probably be your starting point. Don't neglect this value asset; flex your mindset muscles.

Data visualization

Well, we aren't going to escape the fact that we need to talk about data visualization within the four levels of analytics. The reality is, it plays a key part within descriptive analytics. I will speak to data visualization for all three pillars of my tridata, starting now with data-driven problem solving.

A data visualization can be the starting point for your problem-solving work. A data visualization is a brilliant way to build your descriptive analytics. Descriptive analytics is describing the situation, but we don't want to read a massive table of data to find out what is happening, so how do we simplify that? We utilize a data visualization. In that data visualization, we need to capture the "what is happening?" and use it to build out our descriptive analytics. If we want to problem-solve effectively with data, we must have a solid understanding and foundation of what is happening. To help us build our data visualization, let's look at a few steps we can utilize.

These steps or tips are not exhaustive, we need to remember that, and we can find books on building data visualizations. Here, I lay out steps to help you build out a data visualization that can tie back to the business objective effectively. Pick up other great books for the picking of a chart or how to use color appropriately in a visualization. Here are the steps:

1 Know your objective

2 Know your audience

3 Know your tool

4 Know your visualization types

5 Know your story

Let's dive into each of these.

Know your objective

When you are building dashboards, are you working directly towards a goal or objective? What is it that you are building the dashboard for? Yes, I think we all realize we are building it for some reason, but a question that we may ask is how is that objective hitting the team, business unit, or organizational goal? Take the time to study and know your objective for the dashboard.

I think in the world of data and analytics, what we find is that we are doing a lot of work that may not be of a lot of value. At one point in my career, I was speaking with an organization. Now, if I have my numbers right, they had 400 dashboards and were using six of them. You read that right. Six. Now, how does this happen? Why is it we build out these dashboards or visualizations and get to a point where we have 400 and are only utilizing six? I would say not having a clear direction is a key element of this. For descriptive analytics to be effective, we must have that clear objective, that north star we are working towards. Think of the amount of time that could be opened up by not maintaining 400 dashboards; think of the flow of the four levels of analytics that could come to fruition with the freeing of time in this situation.

Know your audience

Have you ever been spoken to and wondered what in the world that person was talking about? Have you ever been speaking and felt, this group does not get a word of what I am saying? There are probably countless examples of dialog or speaking where one side or the other, or both, don't know what in the world the other is saying. Knowing your audience is one of the key things you can do to build a good data visualization and strong descriptive analytics.

Once you know your objective, what you are truly trying to achieve with your data and analytical work, then go into knowing the audience. Is it an audience of one, yourself? Do you have a smaller group, maybe your team you are working on or with? Or is the audience large and you are delivering a webinar, keynote presentation, or breakout session?

Knowing your audience is an absolutely crucial element of building out a strong data visualization. We may know what we like and we can build to that, but if it isn't what your audience likes, they may not react to it as enthusiastically as we would like. Know your audience to help you get buy-in to the descriptive analytic and story you are trying to share.

Know your tool

This may seem obvious, but is it though? How well do we truly know the tools we are using? Some of the tools are Qlik, Power BI, Tableau, and yes, even Microsoft Excel. Maybe you know the tools you use very well, but you need to know the tool well enough to build the data visualization you want. Know the tool's limitations. Know how easy it is for the audience to filter and utilize the visualization effectively. Know how to bring the tool to life for your audience. Unfortunately, as is the case with probably a lot of data and analytics tools, we get caught up in the areas of the tool we like and we may miss out on different features the tool has for us to really bring our descriptive analytic to life. Don't let personal preferences impede the success you can have. Please note, though, that you can utilize your personal preferences in the tool to be successful and drive the descriptive analytic forward. What I am discussing here is the mindset of not allowing yourself to see the openings and opportunities the tool has for you to make your visualization even better.

Know your visualization types

Do you find yourself building descriptive analytic visualizations with the same charts and visualizations? Do you find yourself using the same colors within the visualization? Do your dashboards all look alike?

If you answer these questions in the affirmative, that isn't necessarily a bad thing, especially if you are communicating your story or your descriptive analytic well. What I don't want is for you to miss out on ways to build a visualization that are more effective at driving descriptive analytics and telling the story of what is happening. If there are charts and visualizations you have heard of before but don't know how they work, take the time to invest in yourself and learn. One of the key things a new visualization may do for you is help you see the data in a different light and drive new insight (insight is for the next chapter on diagnostic analytics).

Know your story

Overall, for your data visualization to be the most effective it can be, drive your descriptive analytics by knowing your story. Do you know the context and the problem you are solving? Do you know how you will use your descriptive analytics and do you know how this fits into the problem solving you are doing? Ask yourself questions like: What is the audience I am addressing here (we spoke of this)? What is the business objective or business question we are answering with this descriptive analytic? Have I looked at all the different types of visualizations that are possible for this story? Just question it and see if you know the story. Utilize this to help you with a powerful descriptive analytic through data visualization.

A quick note on asking your questions: don't get caught in analysis paralysis or perfection paralysis. The reality is, we can overthink things. We can overdo it. Let's not let that happen. Let's make sure we learn to be effective AND efficient.

Summary

Data-driven problem solving is a key element to driving descriptive analytics effectively. Having the right mindset and the right data visualization are great ways to help with data-driven problem solving. They can help set the frame and story correctly. Ensure you are developing in these areas effectively.

Descriptive analytics and data-driven decision making

It is one thing to problem-solve and find something within your problem solving, having the "eureka" moment, but then what do you do with it and how does descriptive analytics play a part in that next part? The next part after data-driven problem solving is data-driven decision making. Now, we are not going through a whole treatise on that, there are books out there by Kevin Hanegan[2] or Ben Jones[3] that can teach you the whole process, but how do we bring descriptive analytics into the decision-making process?

Think of descriptive analytics as a tone setter, a foundational piece for your decision making. If we want to know where we are going, we need to know where to start. Utilize the power of storytelling within descriptive analytics to help drive the decision-making process.

If you are not the one making the decision but are helping the decision makers by providing information, use descriptive analytics to tell a short, concise story of what is happening. We can get caught up in providing too much information, too many visualizations, too many descriptive analytics. For the decision-making process, get really good at simplifying your foundational information. Here are my tips to make this happen:

- **Rid yourself of irrelevant information.** Help yourself streamline the data-driven decision making process, get really good at stripping yourself of the unnecessary information that is present within all the descriptive analytics. This can be tough. Do you know what one of the most powerful words within data and analytics is? NO! Yes, the word "no." As you are building the descriptive analytics for the decision-making process, you may find that you can visualize the data 15 ways, but how effective is this? You need to get good at deciphering what is and isn't relevant, what does and doesn't matter. As you do this, simplify the data. We don't need it to be complicated, in fact, that may be bad for us in the decision-making process.

- **Bullet-point the story.** Don't write novels of information that need to be greatly processed by many people. No, that is not the point of descriptive analytics. I recommend you bullet-point the foundational information for your audience or for yourself. As you are building the descriptive analytics that will be utilized by the audience, whether yourself or others, having concise bullets that the audience can use quickly to help frame the decision can be key. Don't try to wax eloquent, but find words that are quick, easy to understand, and rid yourself of the long paragraphs.

- **Highlight the important parts.** Here is a great tip to help bring to life the descriptive analytics necessary for the decision you are trying to make. Are there ways for you to highlight within your descriptive analytics? Can you circle or draw attention to the data points that tell the descriptive analytics effectively?

- **Build towards the audience.** We have shared this in the previous section on data visualization, but the reality is, when you are driving towards the decision-making process, the audience matters greatly. If you are the audience and trying to make a decision with the data, the descriptive analytics will drive your decision and ability to make it matter. The same goes for if you are building towards a different person or group making the decision. Are you driving things toward what will empower them in the decision-making process? If not, you need to do that. To build toward the audience, talk to them, ask them questions, ask them how they want to see data. Ask them what they are truly solving for with this decision and then build the descriptive analytics that will empower them to make the decision. Overall, building towards the audience can be empowering for the decision makers, plus it will help you shine with those you are supporting and helping.

Summary

Overall, descriptive analytics is the foundational data piece for data-driven decision making. This sets the tone and the story of what is happening or has happened. Having this knowledge is key to making a smart data-driven decision. How often are we personally making decisions without all relevant information and the outcome is exactly what we wanted? Now, that said, a word of caution, and one that will sound very familiar to you. Let me ask: do you need *all* the information to make a decision? NO! There is that wonderful word again. The answer is no. You need enough information or you need the information you can get your hands on, but don't expect to have it all or to be perfect. Get comfortable in the uncertainty or in the "I don't have everything" world. Data and analytics isn't perfect, so don't stress if your descriptive analytics don't perfectly address the situation. Build as best you can to show and share with your audience as much of the foundation as you can. Then, work with them or allow them to run with it.

Descriptive analytics and data-driven execution

Data-driven execution is about the execution of a data-driven decision you have made. In our case, descriptive analytics plays a key role in the execution of a data-driven decision because of the importance of descriptive analytics in telling the story and helping build the framework. The idea for execution came from a gentleman named Dan Everett who commented on a LinkedIn post I made. He made a good point that he hoped my data train didn't stop at the decision and he is right. We have to execute well on it.

I feel that the execution of strategy and decisions is hard. As people, we drive back to where we are comfortable, doing what we have always done, and of course, a lot of people don't like change. Data-driven decisions may be all about change: a change in direction, change away from something we have done the same way for years, change away from preconceived notions and gut feel, change to our skill set through upskilling and reskilling. Data-driven execution is about taking the problem solving we have done to come to a data-driven decision and then executing on that decision. So, where does descriptive analytics play a part in the execution of the decision?

To help us understand this, let's think about data-driven execution itself. Is execution of a decision in the business world just a quick process? We have a leader who says "do this" or "do that" and then the decision is done and we move on to the next? Or is execution of a decision a process, one where there could be steps involved? One where we need monitoring of the decision and execution, allowing us to iterate and pivot along the way? I am hoping people answer the latter question in the affirmative here.

The reality is, execution of decisions is a process and in data-driven decision making and data-driven execution, it is no different. Think of data-driven execution as a process where you, whether a data or non-data professional, have the opportunity to utilize descriptive analytics to help along the way.

Think about something you may have been involved in from an execution perspective. How often are you evaluating and thinking on what you are executing? How often are you grouping together with different parties in your organization to evaluate how things are going? How often are you pivoting within the execution of the item you are working on? I think a lot of us would say that we do this often. Take my current case for example.

In the role I currently hold as I write this book, I am helping execute on a data strategy for a new product launch. There are many components to this and we are executing in a process. As such, we have meetings regularly to see where things are and we iterate/pivot as needed. How do you think descriptive analytics can help us along the way? They can help share the story of the progress of the execution you are going through.

Now, for a large project like a data strategy implementation, there are many key elements and pieces along the way. That's fantastic! Bring descriptive analytics to the table. Don't bring lots of long paragraphs, emails, slides with many words. Bring concise and to the point metrics and data and information points to meetings to show progress. One, this can help illuminate all the work your team is involved in and two, this can help to keep the foundational story going, so we see progress and know where we are in the process. Without illumination of status and where we are in the execution of a data-driven decision, we may not know the direction we are going and if it is even the right one.

Again, with all this talk of being data driven, please do not forget the human element in all of this. You have talent, experience, intuition, and gut feel that I want you to bring to the table. But, as I say this, don't go extreme one way or the other. Utilize the data-driven aspect and your human aspect together.

Chapter summary

As I have said, I am writing this book differently than other data and analytics books. You can find books on how to build a better data visualization. You can find a book on how to do coding or analytics or statistics. Instead, we are bringing in this information from the tridata and that is how to get better at the four levels of analytics within data-driven problem solving, decision making, and execution.

In this chapter, we spoke directly of descriptive analytics. I don't need to regurgitate the information here, but remember, utilize descriptive analytics to tell the story of what is happening or has happened. You can also use it to tell the story of future possibilities with predictive and prescriptive analytics. The point is, descriptive analytics should be utilized to describe what is happening. Utilize that in the tridata and use it to really set foundations for you. With the right foundation and context, you can set yourself up for more successful work with the remaining levels of analytics.

CHAPTER DEFINITIONS AND TAKEAWAYS

- **The tridata:** The tridata consists of three things that are needed within data and analytical work, so don't leave things out. You need data-driven problem solving, decision making, and execution.

- **Data and analytics mindset:** A data and analytics mindset is one that is curious, inquisitive, and doesn't just take things at face value. This mindset also is iterative, understanding that you aren't going to get things right from the get-go every single time. No, you need to iterate and have an open mindset.

- **Data-driven problem solving:** Data-driven problem solving is utilizing data to help problem-solve.

- **Data-driven decision making:** Data-driven decision making is utilizing the data to make decisions.

- **Data-driven execution:** We can't just land one cool insight or prediction, we have to execute. Utilize data through the data train and execute on things.

Notes

1 Fandom (nd) Triforce, https://zelda.fandom.com/wiki/Triforce (archived at https://perma.cc/8BSR-JFZF)

2 Hanegan, K (2021) *Turning Data Into Wisdom*, https://kevinhanegan.com/tdiw (archived at https://perma.cc/T2VK-XDGA)

3 Jones, B (nd) Data Literacy, https://dataliteracy.com/resources/ (archived at https://perma.cc/5K4M-FR9M)

7

Diagnostic analytics

What are diagnostic analytics?

We have just concluded three chapters on descriptive analytics and it is time for us to jump forward into what we will call the "why" analytics: diagnostic analytics. Let's take a look at Figure 4.1 of the four levels of analytics.

You may notice that the arrows point back and forth. Yes, you can look at the four levels of analytics as a process. Start at descriptive analytics and work clockwise through the levels. Go from descriptive to diagnostic to predictive to prescriptive. But, don't pigeonhole yourself this way. You can go back and forth and through the levels. Use the system, but work through them effectively and efficiently. Find ways to use all the levels at different times and move forward through your journey. That said, let's get to the topic at hand and speak to diagnostic analytics. What are diagnostic analytics? Let's use an example to help us understand diagnostic analytics more: the housing crash of 2007/08.

The housing crash

The housing crash of 2007/08 was intense and felt for years. In the years before it happened, though, were there signs that the crash could occur? What was the data showing? Could people have known and prevented what was going to happen?

What is interesting about the housing crash is that the data during the boom that led to the crash was like nothing that had been seen in the housing market before; we hadn't had a housing market like that! So, when modeling the housing market and using data from the past for the current market, how effective is that strategy? If we are making apple pie we can't substitute bananas for apples and think it is going to turn out the way we want, and I would argue you can't use data from a different-looking market to predict what will happen in a current market. That is bad gasoline for a predictive modeling fire. What could have been done to prevent that? Well, I won't write a long treatise on the crash, but one question could have helped to drive a conversation that may have helped model better: why are we using prior data that doesn't match our current market to predict what is going to happen? Now, I am not presumptuous enough to say this one question could have prevented what happened, but maybe it would have sparked some conversations and altered modeling and maybe we could have seen what was coming. Again, there are many factors that led to the housing crash, but with a key question, maybe things could have been avoided or at least we could have had more conversations around it. That question is: why?

The question why

This question "why" is a funny one. If you have kids, you may get that question quite often and get sick of it and frustrated (trust me, I know). If you are a data and analytics professional, how often do you like your work to be questioned and looked at by peers? Do you get frustrated by them questioning what you are doing? I will let you in on a little secret: you should be letting them question it left and right. This doesn't mean that your work is wrong or incorrect; it may be 100 percent correct, but questions are a good thing. During my personal training and working out, I should be asking why quite often: Why am I not hitting my goals? Or why am I hitting my goals? Is this training what I need it to be? Why or why not? The question of "why?" may just be the most powerful question in the world and we need to deploy it more in our work. Let's define diagnostic analytics here.

In an article by digitaldirections.com, the definition of diagnostic analytics is basically finding out cause and effect.[1] Essentially it is finding out why something happened. In our previous example, we could turn the table after the housing crash and study the historical data to find out "why" it happened. In marketing, whether we have a successful or unsuccessful campaign, we can find out "why" it was or wasn't successful. If you are looking at product development and you have launched the product, you can find out "why" the launch was or wasn't successful. This understanding of "why" things are or aren't happening is crucial. I put this level of analytics as the most important. This is helping you, your team, your business unit, or your organization succeed at knowing why things are happening. Think of how powerful that is. Knowing why things are happening can help you make smarter decisions. This is also a great alignment between your "hunches" on why things are happening and using the data to combine with your hunches to see if you are correct. It is a powerful thing in data and analytics. We can get caught up in the tools and technologies, but in the end, we need to understand why things are occurring and your hunches and the human element can play a big part in that.

A personal example

It isn't just the business setting where these diagnostic analytics will play a part. Take a look back at my ultra-marathon, the Speedgoat 50k. My dehydration was probably very real and greatly impacted me, but just looking at metrics and saying, "wow, that's good information to have" is only a part of it. Imagine if I was dehydrated like I was, found out how much sweat I had lost, and then, if I ran the race the next year, prepared the exact same way. Could I expect a different result if I went at it in the same manner? I should hope not.

Instead, I should sit down and take the time to understand my preparation and find areas of "why" I struggled so much with my water loss. I need to question myself and my thoughts, my race, my prep leading up to it. Questions are good, always remember that; don't fret over asking questions. During the race, did I get a false sense of it being not too hot because I didn't feel too hot and therefore wasn't sweating too much? Well, obviously, that isn't the case. Did I take into account the shade I was under at times during the race and therefore I was probably very hot, but not realizing it? Was I taking enough salt during the race to not be losing it? In the week leading up to the race, was I eating and drinking the way I should?

One thing to be clear on is that sometimes we don't know the "why" exactly and we won't figure it out. That is ok. We need to be good at testing our ideas, using data to help us, and then reevaluating. We aren't going to be perfect in our efforts to find the "why." Sometimes, yes, we will find it perfectly and know that is why it happened, but I would venture a lot of times we are looking at correlation or thoughts around why, and not finding causation. Remember, correlation does not mean causation. So, with diagnostic analytics, we need to be good at the idea that we are looking at the whys of things occurring and we are testing them, we are iterating on them. Remember, mindset is everything. Having the right mindset of, "this may not be right, but we are going to go at it and see if it is. If not, we will iterate, learning from what we did, and then move forward."

Diagnostic analytics and organizational roles

As we discussed in the previous section on descriptive analytics, let's discuss diagnostic analytics with job roles. When we think of the four levels of analytics, the vast majority of data users will be working within descriptive analytics and diagnostic analytics. Think of Figure 4.1. If we were to divide along the diagonal, from the top left to the bottom right, we could say that 90–99 percent of the users of data in an organization will fall in the upper right half, descriptive and diagnostic analytics. The bottom left half is your more technical data and analytics professionals, predictive and prescriptive analytics. Those in the bottom left could have data and analytics in their titles, or similar.

Diagnostic analytics is the most important area of the four levels of analytics, in my opinion, because it taps into the "why" behind what is happening. Do you see a pattern in the data but wonder why? Your whole organization and all the roles within in it should have some ability to tap into it and understand the why. Now, in some cases, this just means that a person can ask good questions and communicate effectively with the data and analytics professionals who have more technical skills. With the more technical skills, they can then dive in and help you find out the "why."

Overall, never forget that every individual in an organization should have the ability to dig in and help find the "why" in some way. Let's explore the role of data and analytics and how it participates in and helps drive the powerful diagnostic analytics.

Business or end user

This is the most common user of data and analytics. This is also the group of data users who may have the most wide and varying skills within a group of roles. Why is this? Because the end or business user could be one who isn't a data and analytics professional by title or trade, but is skilled in the fields with some degree of proficiency. Then, you have those who are novices in the data and analytics space. Think of a wide spectrum of skills within data and analytics. Now, how does the end user or business user look into data and find insight, to find the "why?"

First, an end or business user will be the recipient or user of descriptive analytics. That is a beginning point of looking to find the insight within the data and analytics.

If we look at Figure 3.1, we can see the data sits at the left of the chart. Data needs the analytics to bring it to life. The analytics lead to insight. The vast majority of the users of data are the end users, those who are trying to utilize the data to find insight to make a decision. One area of my career can illustrate this process.

While I worked at American Express, I helped support the US Consumer Card group, which at the time, and probably still is, the largest portfolio of cards at American Express. In my role I would help lead the buildout of data for end users in that group. Of course, what we built was descriptive analytics. It was then up to the end or business users of the data I was helping to provide to them to find the insight. Herein, though, is where data literacy is a big portion of learning for end or business users. What if those users don't know how to find the insight?

First, those end or business users can learn how to find insight. They can find techniques and ways to find insight in the work. Second, they can network well with data and analytical professionals who may be able to find the insight or help them find it. Herein we see the need for good data fluency within an organization plus the right culture where people are working together, outside of siloes, to help drive data and analytical decisions.

Overall, one of the keys is to ensure that individuals who are end or business users are able to work with the data in a manner that helps them read the descriptive analytics and then to process insight, working towards diagnostic analytics. Here, let's bring the party of data literacy to the table.

Data analyst

With the role of data analyst and how it plays into the world of diagnostic analytics we are now diving into the more technical side of data and analytics. When we think of a data analyst, they play a key role in descriptive analytics as they are building out descriptive analytics and data visualizations for us. That's key for us to be able to find insight and to see and recognize patterns. I mean, how many of us want to look at a table of data that has 50 columns and 50,000 rows of data and be told to find the patterns and insight? I sure hope you aren't answering yes to that! If you are, please reach out to me as there are easier ways to do this. But let's look at two key roles the data analyst plays with diagnostic analytics.

The first role of the data analyst with regard to diagnostic analytics is to build the descriptive analytic that tells us what is happening. A good descriptive analytic should empower a consumer to help them easily tell what is, has, or could be happening.

A data analyst should also be building the data visualization and descriptive analytic in a way that an end or business user can then pull out the insight and see the trends. Remember this if you are a data analyst. You should be building out the descriptive analytics so that the consumer will have an easier time finding the patterns, trends, etc., that can lead to insight and information to help in the data-driven decision-making process. We will discuss how a data analyst can build data visualizations that lead to diagnostic analytics in Chapter 9.

The second way a data analyst works within diagnostic analytics is to be the one digging in and finding the insight itself. Now, what is the difference between a data scientist (we will discuss them next) and a data analyst? Let's keep this simple: skills. Data scientists will have more advanced skills. The way I view it is the data scientist is going to have the skills that work within predictive and prescriptive analytics while a data analyst works more within descriptive and diagnostic analytics.

For a data analyst working within diagnostic analytics, they will be working within descriptive analytics and data to find the trends and patterns to help find the insight.

Data scientist

Now, I just mentioned that a data scientist will work within predictive and prescriptive analytics, as will all users of data, as even those who are business users and data analysts will need to have foundational knowledge of the advanced levels of analytics. They will need to be able to speak the language of predictive and prescriptive analytics, helping to move those forward. The data scientist will have more than foundational knowledge within descriptive and diagnostic analytics. The data scientist will be able to do things within diagnostic analytics to help pull out the insight. For example, a data scientist can work to find the patterns and do statistics to help find statistical significance. This can help to drive knowledge around what may be causing the "what" in descriptive analytics.

Remember, correlation does not mean causation. Because of this, we need to understand we are working to find the "why" behind things, but to truly find full causation may be impossible. We need all of those working within data and analytics to understand and get comfortable with uncertainty. Since correlation doesn't mean causation, what if we can get close to knowing what caused something or have an educated guess? We need to have the right data and analytical mindset that allows us to then assume the "why" and have that get us to make decisions and execute on the data.

If we are looking at the pillars of a data-driven culture, herein is where data scientists and all users of data will use an iterative approach to data and analytics to bring it forward. An iterative approach is where we may not get the right answer the first time, but we don't fail. We learn from what we have done and iterate.

Data engineer and data architect (or any backend data role)

On the backend of data, we have those like the data engineer and data architect. Those who design the backend modeling have a good, valuable, and foundational role within diagnostic analytics. These roles are pivotal because they build the design of the data. If we don't have a strong backend, like a good data warehouse, data lake, or data lakehouse, basically a way that our data is structured that allows the frontend analytical works to pull and use data, then we may just be kissing our data and analytics investments goodbye. We need the clean and strong data to enable the frontend users to build and/or utilize descriptive analytics to then move behind and find the "why." The backend for diagnostic analytics is going to be similar to the backend for descriptive analytics: it sets the tone and the foundation. Don't neglect the roles that make up data management and data architecture.

Leadership

Leadership plays a necessary role within diagnostic analytics. First, leadership should have the ability to spot insight, too. We need a fully data-literate organization that can find the trends, patterns, and insight within the data. Now, leadership probably doesn't have the time to build data engineering and models on the backend. Leadership probably doesn't have the time to build statistical models or code that drives insight. Leadership probably doesn't have the time to do much with data visualizations beyond filtering and looking at the data differently. But, having said all that, and if you are in a leadership position remember this: leadership should be able to look at data and maybe find patterns or curious things within it, and most importantly, leadership needs to get very good at asking questions that can be used to be data driven. For help in getting better at asking questions, I recommend my friend Kevin Hanegan's book, *Turning Data into Wisdom.*[2]

Let's expand on that. If you are in leadership or are not fully skilled in analytical work that can find the insight, get really, really good at asking questions that can be answered by those who are more technical and stronger in those areas. We need better asking of questions through organizations.

Another role that leadership plays within diagnostic analytics and which resides throughout the four levels of analytics is that of investing in the right tools and technology to support diagnostic analytics. Ensure leadership is helping drive towards the right outcome within data and analytics by investing correctly in the right tools. Tools are not strategies but should help empower strategies. Leaders should be data literate enough and well versed enough in the tools and technology to be able to help pick them out. Now, they don't necessarily have to know all about the tools and technology. They may just need to have the right people in the right roles whom they trust and who can help pick the right tools. Proper investment in tools and skill building is a key aspect of leadership within data and analytics.

Tools and technologies

There are varying tools and technologies that can be used within diagnostic analytics. Let's look at a few, either specific tools or concepts.

Business intelligence tools

Business intelligence tools play a good role within diagnostic analytics. These tools help build the foundation through descriptive analytics and they also help drive diagnostic analytics through their design and how they are built. A skilled data professional can help design the business intelligence tools to help the end user, whether a data professional or not, to be able to filter the data to find the patterns, helping to drive questions and insight.

Some examples of these tools are the same that would exist within descriptive analytics: Tableau, Qlik, Microsoft PowerBI, and more.

Coding languages

Coding becomes more prevalent as we work within diagnostic analytics. Coding can allow us to dig into data more specifically than a business intelligence tool does. The reason for this is that a business intelligence tool is set to the rules that are established for the tool, whereas coding allows us the spectrum of data we have access to. One exception to this is if we are using code within the tool to pull different data than was already present in the data pull. Now, specific doesn't necessarily mean smaller. Coding can allow people to pull large or small data sets or information. Using coding can help us drive forward to the insight we desire.

Some examples of coding languages you may learn are structured query language (SQL), Python, or R. You can learn multiple languages or you can focus your energy on just one.

Statistics and probability

Now this is a fun word! Statistics can be a part of the insight within data and analytics. Statistics is fun, it really is. Statology.com teaches the difference between probability and statistics. It shares that probability is about the likelihood of something happening given the data that we already have, and statistics is taking a smaller sample of data and inferring it onto a larger population.[3] Both of these topics can be powerful and help us figure out "why" things are happening.

Chapter summary

Overall, diagnostic analytics to me is the most important of the four levels of analytics. If we don't know why things are occurring, can we build strong predictions? If we don't know why the descriptive analytics are behaving the way they do, are we just reading about what is happening and then guessing why and what to do next? We all need to develop strong and tactical skills within diagnostic analytics. Now, let's see in the next chapter how diagnostic analytics is being used.

CHAPTER DEFINITIONS AND TAKEAWAYS

- **Diagnostic analytics:** Diagnostic analytics is the key level of analytics to me. Why? Because this is the "why" level of analytics. This is the insight level. Descriptive analytics is the observation and diagnostic analytics is why the observation occurred. This is powerful.

- **Diagnostic analytics: the problem:** Diagnostic analytics is to me the most neglected level of analytics. Why? Because descriptive analytics is the easiest level and predictive and prescriptive are the most exciting. The reality is that without knowing why things are occurring, how can we build good predictions? Data literacy is a key investment for diagnostic analytics. Can we empower everyone to be stronger in their data literacy, which they all have some degree of, and teach them how to find insight better?

Notes

1 Digital Directions Team (2022) What is diagnostic analytics? https:// digitaldirections.com/diagnostic-analytics/ (archived at https://perma.cc/ PGL5-MQ8B)

2 Hanegan, K (2021) *Turning Data Into Wisdom*, https://kevinhanegan.com/tdiw (archived at https://perma.cc/9ZPV-6MHA)

3 Zach (2022) Statistics vs. probablity: what's the difference? *Statology*, https://www.statology.org/statistics-vs-probability/ (archived at https://perma.cc/3X5Y-BH32)

8

How are diagnostic analytics used today?

In this chapter, we want to take a look at how diagnostic analytics are being used in the world today. To help us do this, we will be following along with Chapter 5. It would be good, I feel, to follow the examples we have used throughout the chapters on the four levels of analytics. This allows us to see examples go through the four levels and see how outcomes can be achieved through the levels. As we go through these, I want you to think about yourself, your team, and/or your organization and how it can improve within this space of diagnostic analytics. Like I said in the previous chapter, to me, diagnostic analytics is the most important level. Think about these examples and then think of your work. Do you have areas that are like these examples? Do the examples spark ideas for what you can do differently or different areas of the business where you could improve on diagnostic analytics? Let's begin where we did with descriptive analytics: democratization of data.

Democratization of data—diagnostic analytics

I don't need to expand as much on democratizing data within this chapter; I did that back in Chapter 5. In this chapter, let's just discuss how to democratize diagnostic analytics to the masses at an organization. The reality is, democratizing diagnostic analytics is both giving access to tools and technologies and establishing the culture and mindset of the workforce of an organization. Each and every one of us should work on and/or possess skills for finding the insight within data and analytics. Each of us should establish an iterative mindset. We will talk about democratizing the tools and technologies in the next section; let's talk about the right mindset needed for diagnostic analytics. I call this an iterative mindset.

What do I mean by an iterative mindset? Data and analytics, diagnostic analytics, are not perfect. We will make mistakes at times or will not get the result we want, but we need to iterate on it. This type of mindset must be democratized throughout an organization. We will speak more on tips and tricks to do this in the next chapter, but for now, know that the mindset needs to be democratized and leaders must make it known that it is ok to not reach a desired result in the first attempt. What is desired is a learning mindset to push through the data and analytical work, continually finding more and more diagnostic analytics.

Democratization of diagnostic analytics—tools and technology

Like descriptive analytics, the same tools and technologies that will be utilized can be found within diagnostic analytics, with the addition of more tools and technologies. Let's talk about the right skill set to utilize these tools.

Skill set

Within diagnostic analytics, the skill set that is utilized and democratized through an organization is now moving beyond the skills that are utilized for descriptive analytics; we are now getting more advanced. The first thing to discuss, though, is democratizing descriptive analytics with the *right* tools and technology. Coming back to our golf analogy, we are now moving beyond being just a simple beginner golfer. Maybe we are becoming more advanced in our skill, not taking as many mulligans, and we feel we can move beyond the first level of the game. So, we decide to buy better technology. It is the same within diagnostic analytics.

We are moving beyond democratizing skills that just tell us what has happened and we are democratizing the ability to find insight, the why, throughout the organization. If you personally feel your organization is not at this level, that is ok. You can find good data literacy programs and learning for individuals to empower your organization to find better insight and then work through the tridata (we will discuss this in the next chapter on how to get better with diagnostic analytics).

Data strategy

Herein is an interesting part of the data strategy and democratizing out the abilities and finding of insight. We want to ensure that organizations are allowing every individual to have a seat at the data and analytics and the diagnostic analytics table. What would happen if organizations just allow certain people or areas to find the insight within the data? That could be detrimental and here is why.

If we are limiting to a select group of people to find insight, we are limiting ourselves to a smaller number of viewpoints. Now, there may be cases where this matters and in no way am I suggesting we need to ensure there is broad consensus on decisions, but if we limit things we may allow biases to infiltrate our insight finding. Think, what if we only allowed data analysts to find insight? One, we are not democratizing the data well and two, we are only getting their viewpoint. Instead, we want to give everyone the opportunity to use their curiosity, creativity, and critical thinking (my 3 C's of data literacy) to find insight. Having more viewpoints at the table can be good and can allow us to see things we have missed.

Now, again, we can't get caught in analysis paralysis. We don't want to get full consensus from a large group of people. We can get input and ideas from people, but eventually we need to land on insight, what is happening, and make decisions. This is why the data strategy matters so much and why your organization must have a chief data and analytics officer. If you don't have one, get one! Utilize the strategy to set the rules and regulations you want to place on things, who makes the decisions, etc., but ensure you encourage the whole organization to feel empowered to find insight within the data and information your organization possesses.

Diagnostic analytics—data visualization

Within Chapter 5 on descriptive analytics, we discussed data visualizations. We defined them as the visualization of data elements into different charts and graphs, simplifying it for the non-advanced data and analytics users. This was a summarized version of Tableau's definition.[1] So, how do organizations utilize data visualizations to find diagnostic analytics? The data visualization can be essential.

Dashboards—beyond descriptive analytics

Within diagnostic analytics, we don't want to have to find trends, patterns or insight by looking at massive amounts of data. So, organizations can use dashboards to drive diagnostic analytics by putting the large data sets in simplified format within data visualizations. Then, individuals who are using the data visualization can filter and manipulate (not manipulate in a bad way) the data to see it from different vantage points. This is power. I don't like just seeing a table of numbers. What I want to see is a way for me to filter, change, and dig into the numbers. We need to simplify the large data sets we own so that people can find the insight. Without simplifying, we may not find insight or could find the wrong insight. Let's make sure we as organizations and individuals are working hard to make it as easy as possible to find insight.

One-off data visualizations

Let's turn back to Chapter 5 where we described the pandemic and one-off data visualizations. The same thing can happen with diagnostic analytics. As we drive to find out "why" things are happening, guess what, we really needed to figure out "why" things were happening within the pandemic. Now, we aren't writing this book to describe how good and accurate visualizations were, but let's make sure we are talking about the one-off visualizations. In the pandemic, we could build one-off visualizations to see what was happening and then use them to drive questions that could help to find the why. They could also be used to ask if we could visualize things differently and find better insight. That is key to what we do: is this visualization serving the purpose of helping us find the why or can we change it? Remember the iterative mindset.

Diagnostic analytics—coding

We spoke of coding in the previous chapter, but organizations can help drive insight with diagnostic analytics through coding. No matter the language that is being used, and that should be one that serves the purposes of the data strategy, you should be using the language to drive insight and strong analytical work (if we are doing diagnostic analytics). The coding will drive toward the purpose we want. In our case, we can build set codes that may pull data regularly for us, and that could drive diagnostic analytics. In other cases, it might be an ad hoc pull that is needed.

In my current role as I write this book, I have a data engineer on my team who will handle requests that come through and he then may build code to pull the data. Now, most of the time, if not all the time, he is pulling data that will represent descriptive analytics, but this can spark questions again that can drive the work to find the insight. Sometimes, the one-off code can be used to find out why things are occurring. Then the code is being utilized to fulfill the insight request.

Diagnostic analytics—statistics

We have spoken a bit on statistics, but statistics is one way diagnostic analytics is used today. Now, obviously this is not a skill that is democratized through an organization. Statistics is used by the more technical and professional data and analytics employees, but, through data literacy and data fluency, an entire organization can speak to and through statistics.

Industry examples—continued from Chapter 5

To end this chapter, we will continue the examples from Chapter 5. This will allow us to progress through the overall story of the four levels of analytics, utilizing the same examples.

Healthcare

To help us with the examples we used in Chapter 5, I will copy pieces over for us to refer to and drive our diagnostic analytics. In that chapter and with reference to healthcare, we spoke about utilizing dashboards at a hospital to show how many beds the hospital has and how many are occupied. Another area we explored was watching the trends of an illness as it permeates throughout a region. We mentioned Covid-19 specifically. So, with these let's explore how diagnostic analytics works.

For the first one, we looked at the number of hospital beds that exist and how many are occupied. Why might it be important to understand why people are in the beds? From a diagnostic analytics perspective, this understanding can help with forecasting the number of beds available. If an illness is raging through a community, it can become very important to know why people are in beds to predict how long they will be there and then forecast the hospital's ability to handle the raging illness.

The second example was Covid-19. Of course, knowing the "why" behind things happening with a virus that is new to the world is very, very important. Now, Covid-19 was an example of the iterative mindset. Was everything shared out about it always accurate? Maybe not, but it gave a chance to iterate. It was learning on the go and that is powerful.

Retail

In Chapter 5 we spoke about how retailers like Target and Walmart can utilize descriptive analytics to understand inventory and when to supply or stock again. We also spoke about how retail businesses can utilize descriptive analytics to understand busy times and seasons and then the number of employees and number of hours needed.

For the retail industry, diagnostic analytics could be the difference between losing, making profit, or making big profit. Think of the first example of descriptive analytics I had in place, to understand supply and demand, what is happening in the economy, etc., and why it can lead to a smarter strategy for what to stock and when.

In the second example I used around the number of employees to have in the place of employment and the hiring practices, knowing what is happening and why can help to empower smarter data-driven decisions. Sometimes seasonality can kick in, like with my family member. In some cases, the understanding of "why" could lead to a stronger understanding of the workforce and the employees of the company.

Marketing

Here is what we wrote about the marketing industry in Chapter 5: marketing can utilize descriptive analytics to show what is happening in a campaign. This is powerful and needed information. We don't want to just play the guessing game on what is happening. We want to utilize the descriptive analytics to show us. Marketing can also use descriptive analytics to understand the demographics of their customer base. Again, it is powerful to know demographic information and not be guessing. We did emphasize that we cannot use the descriptive analytics to build campaigns that would be discriminatory.

The "why," diagnostic analytics, may be the most important thing for marketing in general. Think about that one for a second and ask yourself, why did the author say that? Set the book down and think about it... The reality is, knowing why campaigns are and aren't working is a powerful way to build and drive your marketing. If we know why people are or aren't attracted to our products because of our marketing, we can shift the direction of the marketing, putting a better product and marketing campaign forward. If we don't understand why or why not, then, well, we may be throwing spaghetti against the wall and hoping something sticks. In marketing, analytics, especially diagnostic analytics, should be the bedrock of campaigns and campaign design. In the next chapter, we'll jump into some techniques that teach us how to get better at diagnostic analytics and, if you are a marketer, will hopefully help you to get better at your craft.

Finance, financial services, and banking

In Chapter 5 I shared my experience in building descriptive analytics for write-off rates and delinquencies. This was important for American Express to know as my time working on this was after the great financial crisis. We also discussed the use of descriptive analytics to understand products and which are popular and which are not.

From my personal work, the understanding of write-off and delinquency rates was very important. When I had that role, the US economy was still struggling from the housing crisis that hit it in 2007/08. To know what was happening, descriptive analytics was very important, and knowing why it was happening could be all the more crucial. The understanding of why it was happening could help drive my company to know what to predict next. As part of the data, as I recall, I think the predictive analytics were already built and I inherited the report. The data showed what was happening and where the month could end up. The "why" could help the organization and those needing this data make decisions. Now, herein is a key point: not all data needed to understand the "why" will come from inside the company. External data can play a key role. External data can be sourced, such as just reading the news and what is happening in the world's economies. In this case, external data helped us to understand what was happening in the economy, and whatever other data could empower those wanting to know "why" to understand it.

The other thing I wrote about in Chapter 5 for this industry was a knowledge of the products and what is and isn't popular. This is something that can span across different industries: Why don't people like our products or this specific product? If we change it this way, will it help? Which are our most popular products and what is it about those products that makes them popular? Overall, understanding the "why" behind the products and their popularity can help drive product design and improve an organization's ability to sell its products and services. If we don't get why, we may make changes and designs that actually crush a popular aspect of a product and lose sales because of it. Surveys can be problematic within data and analytics because answers could be used to game the survey towards what one thinks may be desired, or one might be biased. With surveys, make sure they are designed right, but qualitative data may be powerful in helping push forward diagnostic analytics on products.

Supply chain and logistics

What we wrote for supply chain and logistics was short, but it matters: "Having descriptive analytics to understand the logistics and supply chain of your organization or of the global economy is very important."

Think about the Covid-19 pandemic. Think of supply chain and logistic problems in general. Having descriptive analytics of both an internal and external data perspective can help to know the story, but then the "why" can empower us to find solutions and push past problems or improve upon already well-running situations. When we see supply chain issues and we can figure out "why," like maybe knowing that shut-downs during the pandemic were causing problems, hopefully we can see beyond them and push to success. In some cases, though, even when we know or have a good idea on the diagnostic analytics, patience is needed because we may not be able to move beyond it quickly or effectively; we may be stuck for a time.

A side note on this: don't get caught up in a thought process that data will drive answers quickly. Patience truly is a virtue. Sometimes, and I can think of Covid-19 as one example, we are very quick to bring data forward but then it is wrought with problems. Be patient, watch for signs, think deeply on things and use the third C of data literacy: critical thinking. Don't think that data will give you quick and perfect decisions. Yes, we don't want to bog ourselves down and be too slow, but we don't want to be too fast. Both can have negative impacts or consequences. Instead, patiently and intelligently work through the data and analytics at your table and make smart, purpose-filled data-driven decisions and then execute on them.

Data ethics and diagnostic analytics

With diagnostic analytics, how do we ensure we are using data ethically? One key area here is to be objective and open that the data may show unethical practices or other things within it. If we find the "why" is leaning towards one key area or demographic but is ignoring others, are we open enough to see the "why" and communicate it out? If not, then we need to ensure the ethical use of data when we see things that look off.

Another area we need to ensure within the ethical use of data is to remove our personal bias. This doesn't always tie across into unethical use, but sometimes we are looking for our own answers in the data versus objectively looking for answers. As organizations are using data today, we need to ensure the ethical use of data and the ethical finding and use of diagnostic analytics—the "why".

Chapter summary

Diagnostic analytics is power, without a doubt. Knowing "why" things are occurring or having good ideas on it should empower us to make smarter decisions. Whether that be in our personal lives or in our careers or our organizations themselves. Knowing what is happening and following up with why it is happening can be key to driving a business, career, or our personal lives forward. Look for ways in your career and personal life in which you can figure out "why" things are happening, more and more and more. Then, utilize the "what" and the "why" to make better decisions.

As you can see in this chapter, when an organization knows why things are happening, better decision making can occur. When organizations are making better decisions, they are better organizations. Now, let's see how we can improve in these areas.

CHAPTER DEFINITIONS AND TAKEAWAYS

- **Democratization of diagnostic analytics:** Diagnostic analytics should be used by everyone. Does this mean that everyone needs advanced technical skills to drive statistics or advanced levels of diagnostic analytics? Of course not! But everyone should be inquisitive and be able to ask questions of the data. Now, you may not need to be the one who digs in deeply to the data, no. But you can be the one who asks a good question that the data and analytics professionals can dig into. So, you may just become good at asking questions and that is great. Utilize your ability to ask powerful questions and drive analytical work.

- **Diagnostic analytics: multiple uses:** Utilize the powerful resources at your disposal to drive diagnostics. Diagnostic analytics is utilized in various ways in the world today.

Note

1 Tableau (nd) What is data visualization? Definition, examples, and learning resources, https://www.tableau.com/learn/articles/data-visualization (archived at https://perma.cc/J2M9-VZEZ)

9

How individuals and organizations can improve in diagnostic analytics

We have discussed what diagnostic analytics is. We have discussed how it is being used. Now, let's discuss how individuals and organizations can improve and get better at diagnostic analytics. With this, the first thing I want to discuss is something that can span across individuals and organizations, but it will be utilized differently. First, let's talk about the individual side of this.

Data and analytics mindset—individuals

Diagnostic analytics is the insight level of analytics. Remember, diagnostic analytics is finding why things are happening. Now, we need to understand that we won't necessarily always get to 100 percent perfect on why something happened. We can get close, but we may not be able to get perfectly there, and that is ok. We need to make sure we are comfortable with that uncertainty. This is part of the mindset we need to be developing. If we develop this mindset, we are improving in our individual abilities with diagnostic analytics.

How can we get better at having a mindset of being comfortable with the uncertainty on our why? This goes back to an iterative mindset. Here is one way you can improve in your diagnostic analytics capability: develop a mindset to test, experiment, and be comfortable with only part of the answer. If we are seeking to be fully 100 percent convinced that we have the "why" behind something, we may still be searching for the "why" for years to come. Instead, come up with guesses and test and experiment on those guesses. That is a great way to improve your comfort with uncertainty: test it out.

As an individual, work and try to build and develop more and more your natural data analytic experimentation. I feel that fear overtakes us more often than it should. Whether that be fear of being wrong, fear of others seeing that your response isn't exactly what it needs to be, fear that you will experience retribution, or working on something that didn't turn out the way you had hoped. This is another way you can improve on your data and analytics mindset and diagnostic analytics: let go of the fear and work toward the understanding that you are iterating and learning as you go.

Finally, I want you to improve in one specific but broad way: be more curious! OK, this is one of my three C's of data literacy. Be more and more curious. Ask lots of questions. Ask "why" all the time. I mean, you are trying to find the "why," so maybe you should ask why much more often:

- Why did we use this visualization?
- Would another visualization work better?
- Did you look at the data in this way?
- I wonder why this person's sales are up while this person's are down?
- I wonder why this product is reacting the way that it is in the market and this one is reacting in a completely opposite way?
- I wonder if we changed this up, would people be more productive?

Asking questions is a good thing and can spark work within diagnostic analytics. We need to be more and more curious.

Now, there is a caution with this. Don't be curious to a fault. Don't ask so many questions that you turn your coworkers off you or turn them off data and analytical work. Instead, be smart, strategic, think through your questions well, and know your audience well. Knowing your audience can be a good thing when asking questions because it can help you to frame your questions better for the intended person. Now, what about organizationally?

Data and analytics mindset—organizations

Organizations can develop an "organization" mindset when it comes to what I spoke about with regard to individuals. We need to celebrate the wins and losses. For organizations, the mindset they need to adopt for all levels of analytics is one of iteration and that when we aren't all the way there with knowing the "why," that is ok and we can push forward with our work. This may be a shift for an organization and its leaders. A lot of times, people like certainty, they want to know things are certain and in the right spot. Well, at times with data and analytics, we aren't certain. We need leaders to support and uphold this mindset that we are ok with the uncertainty. We are ok if we are only partially there. We are ok if we aren't 100 percent accurate but we iterate and move forward. Ensure your organization is adopting this mindset.

Another mindset that an organization needs to develop is that of allowing questions about everything. Again, we are not talking questions that push us to a level of annoyance but questions that help move the mission and vision of an organization forward. What a powerful thing it is for an organization to allow questions throughout. Ask yourself: do members of your C-suite or executive team welcome their numbers and data being questioned? If not, then we may need to work on that mentality with them a bit. We want them to be comfortable if the most junior employee in the company comes up and says to them, "hey, I may have a better way of looking at that data than what you presented, can I show it to you?" or, "hey, why did you use that visualization, did you know it may come to life more for your audience or for finding insight if we use this visualization?" The reality is, we should be fostering a culture of questioning like this, allowing everyone to feel a part of it.

The more an organization allows questioning to flow through it, the more empowered it can be to understanding the "why" behind things. Imagine you are missing something because you are not comfortable with your work or ideas being questioned. In reality, we should all want people to poke holes intelligently at our work and what we are doing, allowing for further discussion and more eyes on our work. That is a powerful way to drive forward the data and analytical work we want to occur through the four levels of analytics.

Note, these types of mindset changes are not going to happen overnight but can help empower an organization to further success. Take the time to implement these, to truly develop them, and to work toward those pieces of insight you are looking for.

Diagnostic analytics and the tridata

OK, now let's turn back to what I did with descriptive analytics in Chapter 6. Remember, there are already books on fundamental skills for diagnostic analytics. I may touch upon some of those in this area, but I want to turn our attention back to the tridata itself and utilize diagnostic analytics to improve the key elements therein: data-driven problem solving, decision making, and execution. Let's jump in with data-driven problem solving.

Diagnostic analytics and data-driven problem solving

This actually might be the essence of diagnostic analytics: data-driven problem solving. Here is why. When we are running data and analytical work in our lives, personal or business, to really improve in our decision making, we must figure out "why" things are occurring. When we are kids growing up in school, when we are adults figuring things out, what we are doing can be called problem solving.

A definition of this comes from ASQ and, to paraphrase, it is: defining a problem, coming up with proposed ideas and solutions, evaluating those solutions and selecting one, and then implementing and iterating back.[1]

This definition sounds similar to what I teach when I speak. We must go through a process and iterate on that process. Now, think about this definition with regard to diagnostic analytics—I want you to think about how you can improve on this.

First, one way you can improve in your diagnostic analytics work with regard to problem solving is to bring new ideas to light. As the definition from ASQ teaches us, we are coming up with proposed ideas and solutions. How often do we revert back to our old ways of doing things? How often do we revert back to our old ways of thinking? Where we are comfortable? Shame on us for doing this! Data and analytics should be something that helps illuminate for us new ideas, new thoughts, and new ways of doing things. This may come to be in no more important area of data and analytics than in diagnostic analytics. Our ability to come up with new ideas is paramount for diagnostic analytic success. What do I mean by new ideas and how does that tie to diagnostic analytics?

Diagnostic analytics is the "why" behind things, as I have probably said more than is necessary in this book. If we are just digging into old ideas that people recognize, know, and are comfortable with, we are not shifting the paradigm. We are not bringing in a new way to see things, a new thought process toward things, so we may just be reinforcing things that occurred in the past. Within data and analytics, we must get comfortable with creating the future and understanding the "why." Now, please note, this doesn't mean that the "why" is something from the past, something we have seen before; don't limit your ideas and proposals for solutions to things that have occurred in the past. Open the door to new possibilities. What can we do to expand our understanding and come up with new proposals to empower our diagnostic analytics and to drive our data-driven problem solving? Here is a list of tips:

1 Set a rule for yourself that within your proposed solutions, two of them are things that are new and different. Make this a hard and established rule. I don't care if these proposals are so out of left field that they may not even have a chance of being a possibility. But what you have done here is created the opportunity for possibility

and I love it. If you see a marketing campaign has been successful, I don't care if the solution is, "the new Marvel movie has people excited about x, y, z, and I think that is one possibility why the marketing campaign was successful." Tying a marketing campaign's success to the newest Marvel movie, well, I am not sure that has anything to do with it but you are now thinking outside the box for potential ideas and solutions to the "why."

A note on this. Get good at recognizing and understanding spurious correlation. Spurious correlation is where two variables are correlated but one is not influencing the other. Think of spurious correlation as "random chance." So, if you come up with something out of left field and then there is strong correlation, please take a step back and reflect on it. I love the quote from the book *Snow Leopard* from Category Pirates which, summarized, says that we need to think about thinking and that is the best kind of thinking.[2] Meaning, think on what you are thinking about. Don't take it at face value but reflect and use what Cal Newport calls deep work.[3] If we just take things at face value and assume they are correlated, we may march down a black hole and not find the success we want. Please watch for correlations, relationships between variables, and reflect and ask yourself, "Does this truly make sense?"

2 Enlist the help of others. You have many in your organization who have different ideas, thoughts, experience, backgrounds, and they may be able to break an "idea block" (think of it like writer's block… you may have "idea block," where you can't think of new ideas). Remember, everyone has a seat at the data and analytics table—are you inviting them to sit at your table? Let them in. Fill them in on the problem you are solving and the data you have obtained or are thinking of obtaining. Let them offer ideas and in no way tell yourself anything is a dumb idea… ever! If we want to create the community we need for data and analytical success, people should feel free to express ideas and proposals on why things are occurring without the fear that they will be made to feel dumb, that their idea couldn't possibly be true. Take their ideas

and, as the Category Pirates teach, think on what you are thinking about. Then, see if it makes sense.

3 Ready to think out of the box? If you can't think of new ideas, go for a walk, step away from what you are doing, and then come back to it. First, taking a walk enables blood flow and the crossing of things in the brain, meaning the left to right sides of the brain. Let things go through, let them flow in you. Here is a story from my career.

Years ago, while I was at American Express, I had a code that wasn't working and I couldn't figure out why. I don't know how long I spent on it before but it was probably too long. Eventually, I stepped away and came back to find it was an error with an extra or missing, I don't remember exactly, comma or semicolon. It wasn't that the code was poor but that I had missed something (if I remember right, this was a long, long code, so finding that wouldn't have been the simplest and it was maybe compounded because I had been looking at it for so long).

Take a step away—no really, please take a step away. Remember, I am not writing this book with the four levels of analytics in the traditional sense. You can find those books out there. Instead, I hope this molds and shapes the mindset and some "other" skills necessary for you to be more successful within data and analytics. I really like this one of taking a break and walking away. Sometimes, we just need to break away and come back to things. If you have no idea how to dig into the diagnostic analytic more, just take a break, go chat with someone, call your friend, parent, partner or spouse, and get your brain away from it.

4 Write things down and just work. Yep, just start writing down your proposals and ideas. Just start to ideate. If you just sit here and edit, edit, edit, or aren't moving forward, just move forward. I was in a meeting within my company, just the week of me writing this, and we were talking about our new business model and product. One person asked a question along the lines of getting the product to the point where it was ready. Well, how do we define ready? We need to not wait until we are "ready," we need to be

natural experimenters and working toward the success we want. Just move. Write ideas down and start experimenting.

With the ideation aspect of data-driven problem solving, that is not the end. We can't just create and come up with ideas and think, "yay, we made it!" No. We need to then problem-solve. We need to dig in and work with it.

Within diagnostic analytics, one way to do this is to start experimenting. Just start testing ideas. If you have an idea, just start digging in. If you don't have ideas, start to think and create them. We need to then dig in. This is the analysis part of diagnostic analytics. Here are a few steps or things we can do to problem-solve on the information:

- First, gather the data you need. You already have your ideas and proposals, well, what data do you need to answer those ideas and proposals? Is it multiple data sets? Is it both internal (data within your organization) and external (data outside your organization) that will help you? Good, go and get that data. Here, you need to let your data literacy skills come to life and if you aren't a data engineer, data analyst, or in a role that has direct access to data, work with those who do. Have them help you grab the new data you need to answer your proposals.

- Build a data visualization on the idea you have. You can utilize tools like Tableau and Qlik to build your data visualization. If you have already looked at a descriptive analytic and seen what happened, you can now visualize the data in a different way and start to build it out. Utilize the power of multiple types of visualizations and add filtering capability to them, so you can see things from a different perspective.

- Within your work, you can form a hypothesis for each of the ideas and proposals you came up with. Then, you need to test those hypotheses and iterate... back to our iterative mindset.

How might we test these hypotheses within the work we are doing? Here is where you utilize your data and analytics "detective" skills. First and foremost, be honest with yourself if you don't know how to dig in and find answers to fill this skills gap. Find books, learning courses, the things you need to improve on. Also, if you don't feel you have the skills, this is where your network can come into play. Do you have good relationships with the data analysts or data scientists in your organization or business unit? Turn to them and find ways to collaborate and find answers together. Having multiple minds on the proposed solutions can be a good thing.

With our newly discovered "solutions" or "whys" we can then proceed to the next part of our tridata with data-driven decision making.

Diagnostic analytics and data-driven decision making

We cannot just sit on our problem-solving skills and the proposed solutions we have come up with. We must decide on what we are going to do. This is crucial. I have seen where data visualizations are made up to be all pretty and cool, but what value do they truly bring except to show what possibilities there are with data and a tool? But, I say, who cares? We need to get value from things to make decisions. Now, in all fairness, if the proposed purpose of the visualization is just to build a cool visualization or to practice and learn new skills from the data viz practitioner, then awesome. But, if you are looking at being truly data driven in an organization, we must problem-solve and then we must come to a decision. The next section will dig into the execution of the decision.

Since diagnostic analytics is primarily focused on the data-driven problem-solving portion of the tridata, this section will be shorter. The key to developing better skills with diagnostic analytics and decision making is to do just that, make a decision. I fear that far too often we are looking to get group consensus on a problem or matter. We want to make sure everyone is on board and supportive. Well, guess what, sometimes people won't agree with decisions and that is ok. Yes, we can get input on the decision we are looking to make, but what we need to do is truly lead on the decision. Here are our proposed solutions. We broke them down, found the "why," thought about our thinking, and from this we have concluded this is our decision. Remember, you can get buy-in but don't wait for full consensus from the group. People can disagree, but teach and help them develop the iterative mindset that says this may not be right, you are correct, but if we wait too long we may have crushed any possibility of a positive outcome. We are going to march forward here, study, learn as we go, and iterate. We are making this decision.

This could be an example of analysis or perfection paralysis. We want to be effective and efficient, and when we have the right mindset and culture in an organization, we know that just because we disagree with a decision doesn't mean it is final. On the contrary, we have the right data-driven mindset that allows us to have differing ideas and the ability to iterate and keep going. With the right mindset, the organization is continually progressing forward and marching. This is key. While I may think that diagnostic analytics is the most important level, that doesn't mean it is perfect.

Diagnostic analytics and data-driven execution

The final phase of our tridata is data-driven execution. I may have spoiled the material of this section in the last section, but just execute on the data-driven problem solving and decision you have made. You have gone through and found ideas. You have tested and analyzed those ideas. You have thought about your thinking. You have then, with efficiency, decided on what you are going to do. Now, it is time to execute.

Through the decision-making process, it should be decided how you are going to execute on this:

- What is it you are going to do?
- Who needs to be involved?
- What teams and people?
- What systems, if any, do you need to execute on this decision?
- What is the timeline you will execute on?

- When do you feel the end of this decision, if any, will take place?
- When will you evaluate?

These are all questions for you to answer in the decision-making process and then you just need to implement the plan.

Execution is about doing and not thinking or talking about doing. I hate being in meetings or organizations where we just talk about stuff and there is a lot of fluff but no execution or strategy to execute. We need to start executing. Just march forward with your ideas and decision. Then, we of course iterate and our wonderful data and analytics train marches forward.

A note on learning

As I have said in this book, I am not writing this in the traditional sense but in a non-traditional data sense. So, I want to add a word about learning about different skills and methodologies for data visualization, analytics, statistics, hypothesis testing, etc. If those are the skills you are looking for, partner them to this book. Both skills are necessary and there are books out there that you can pick up for your analytical skills learning. Think of this book as about the mindset skills with regard to the four levels of analytics work and then the other books as about the technical skills. A proper marriage or partnership between the learning of the two is the right approach to improving your skills within the four levels of analytics.

Chapter summary

To me, the most important level of the four levels of analytics is diagnostic analytics. It is the "why" level of analytics. It is when we are figuring out what is causing things, at least in theory. Remember, correlation does not equal causation, but don't get caught thinking you must get things perfect. No, instead find different solutions, proposals, and "whys" and act on them. Remember the quote from Category Pirates in *Snow Leopard* about thinking.

Now, let's jump from the "why" to the prediction in the next section of chapters: predictive analytics.

CHAPTER DEFINITIONS AND TAKEAWAYS

- **Diagnostic analytics and mindset:** With diagnostic analytics, I want you to develop a very curious mind. We need to be able to find out why things are happening. Now, this begs the question: can we perfectly understand why things are happening? No, probably not. Plus, we don't want to get caught up in analysis paralysis or perfection paralysis. We want to have a mindset to drive and run with what we are understanding, but also have in our mindset that we may be wrong and that is ok. We learn from it.

- **Diagnostic analytics and the tridata:** The tridata has power within diagnostic analytics, especially when it comes to data-driven problem solving. I think of problem solving as a key element to diagnostic analytics. We want to problem-solve and drive answers. We want to understand what is happening. With the why known, we can make decisions and then we can execute on those decisions. We can get and should get good at data-driven problem solving, especially as it pertains to diagnostic analytics.

Notes

1 ASQ (nd) What is problem solving? https://asq.org/quality-resources/problem-solving (archived at https://perma.cc/9NET-45KL)

2 Category Pirates (2022) *Snow Leopard: How legendary writers create a category of one*, https://categorypirates.substack.com/p/snow-leopard-how-legendary-writers (archived at https://perma.cc/T4D7-9G6A)

3 Newport, C (2016) *Deep Work*, https://www.calnewport.com/books/deep-work/ (archived at https://perma.cc/7NC8-B9T8)

10

Predictive analytics

What are predictive analytics?

We have covered descriptive and diagnostic analytics, now let's get to an area that may be seen as a more powerful or shinier area of data and analytics: predictive analytics. Please refer back to Figure 4.1.

Once we have moved past what is happening, descriptive analytics, and we have our ideas about why it happened, diagnostic analytics, we are able to move on to predictive things. This should make sense. Let's turn back to our doctor analogy. The doctor can tell us what is happening and why it is happening. Now, the doctor can tell us what to do to get better. That is a good thing. None of us, at least I hope not, want to live in ill health in perpetuity. It's the same thing in a business setting or with our personal goals. We know what is happening, for good or bad, and we want to improve, drive more revenue, get more customers, whatever that outcome may be. We want to make predictions that allow us to then figure out what happened after the prediction, why it happened, and then return with more predictions, and our wonderful cycle continues. See, this is how we should be working with data and analytics, and this is the mindset we should be deploying in our data and analytical work. We should have the mindset of continuous improvement over time, continuous progress. Let us take a look at a real-world example as I am writing this.

In the last quarter of 2022, in the United States, there is much talk of a recession. Are we already in a recession (which would be a descriptive analytic)? Why are we in such tough times (which would be a diagnostic analytic)? Or if we aren't in a recession, will we get into one (which would be a predictive analytic)? There are probably a lot of thoughts within people's minds around the next little while in time and whether we are in a recession and whether the rough times will impact them. We are hearing about layoffs occurring on what may seem like a daily basis. Herein we can see the importance of understanding predictive analytics and making smart decisions. Here is an example of why good data management, clean data, and smart understanding of how to model and execute on data matter for making smart predictions in your business and in the overall economy as a whole. It matters. Making smart predictions can literally impact lives.

Delinquency and write-off rates

Back to my example of my time working at American Express. One of the things I did within my role that helped build analytics for delinquency and write-off rates was build some predictive analytics. I had a report that I took from being over 70 PowerPoint slides long and broke it down into six total charts. These six charts had descriptive analytics on what was happening in the given month and then had predictive analytics on where the month could end up. This was a powerful way of visualizing things for those who were receiving the report. The chart was showing, "hey, this is what is happening in the given month, and this is where it could end up."

Now, this is also something to understand within predictions and modeling like this: just because something COULD end up there doesn't mean it will. Think about the pandemic for me. How many organizations had "pandemic" in their 2020 forecasts? I am guessing 0 percent or at least probably very close to that. Then what happened? The world felt like it shut down.

With regard to the delinquency and write-off rates, we could see the predictions, but what if there was something in the data we didn't know about? What if there was something in the economy that hadn't hit the model yet? This is a part of the data and analytical mindset: knowing that predictions can go awry and miss the mark, knowing there may be something in the data we don't know about, and it could pop our prediction off and out the window. Developing this data and analytical mindset, this ability to pivot and shift and understand the data and its gaps, can help you be successful with predictive analytics. It is a part of the iterative journey and can take the predictions further and better.

Weather

Another example of predictive analytics, and one where we see predictions quite frequently, especially if you check it often, is the weather. A recent example that happened to me during the writing of this book shows weather predictions and choices I made because of the weather.

In November 2022 I had a trip to Florida to do a data workshop, but there was one problem leading up to my travel: a late hurricane was coming towards Florida. Me being new to hurricanes, I was worried. Given the potential of the hurricane and a snowstorm in my state, I decided to adjust the travel and leave a day earlier. I also changed my flight on the way home. I am grateful for predictions and the ability to shift my travel.

Overall, the weather is one we see all the time. Weather reporting uses predictions to show us the potential of what the weather will be. Do they always get it right? No, of course not, and let's be honest, have you ever been frustrated with weather predictions? I would say a lot of people have been frustrated there. But please give those who build weather predictions a lot of credit. From the book *The Signal and the Noise* by Nate Silver, I learned that weather predictors deserve more credit than we give them.[1]

Ultra-marathon running

OK, this example is a personal one, but data and analytics is not just for business— you can also use it in your personal lives. Also, hopefully through the personal or organizational examples I give, you are learning how you may be able to do things differently.

For me, the killer race was the Speedgoat 50k. Using my knowledge of the descriptive analytics I was given, plus then figuring out some potential "whys," I can work my fitness and training into the 2023 race, if I decide to do it. Using our abilities to decipher through things and find potential answers, that is key. Then, do not forget to make predictions and then test those predictions.

One thing to note: you can make predictions all you want, but you'd better have a system to analyze and check on those predictions, see how they performed. Then, you can build new descriptive and diagnostic analytics, then new predictions. For me, fitness is such a key part of my life, I personally should get much better at collecting and analyzing my fitness data and making predictions.

Marketing campaigns

Wouldn't it be nice to work in marketing and have a crystal ball that told you all the wonderful things that would occur through your marketing campaign and teach you how to build the perfect campaign? Who to target? How to target them effectively and within the bounds of the law? What things to include and exclude? What language should you use? All of these wonderful things. OK, so, for the small price of $59.95, I have the magic solution for you... OK, do not buy into "snake oil."

The crystal ball doesn't exist, now does it? Of course not. Instead, we need to get good at the data and analytics train, moving forward at a strong and effective pace. Using predictive modeling in marketing campaigns is a powerful and strong way to drive the campaign, using data to be a data-driven marketing organization. Use your descriptive analytics and diagnostic analytics to understand previous marketing campaigns, and then build predictive modeling on projecting out the future. Be very smart and calculated within your descriptive and diagnostic analytics, so you may be empowered within your predictive analytics.

Maybe your marketing campaign is centered on retention of existing customers, so should you build predictions on how the campaign will drive net-new customers to the company? No! Now, don't get me wrong, have an open mind to understanding potential impacts and side-effects of your campaign, for both good and bad, but direct the predictions towards the business outcome you are looking to achieve.

Customer usage

In my current company, customer usage of both our product and the products of the enterprises we are helping matters. If more individuals are using the software—and by using, I mean effectively using and not just getting into the software—then hopefully we are seeing strong adoption of the software. The reverse is also true. So, driving software usage and adoption matters.

If we are enabling data-driven decisions, then the work I am doing in the data space will help my company and our partners to be more successful:

- Can I pull in the relevant factors that help to enable software adoption?
- What conversations can I be having with our partners to help understand what data points matter?
- Am I building the data in a way that will help to illuminate the patterns and trends that will help us to make impactful predictions?
- Am I working in such a way as to communicate with the necessary parties the relevant data and information to help us all understand just what in the world is going on?

Here, we see multiple questions that can be answered to help us be more data driven and more impactful. We need our predictions to be powerful, we can't just "hope" that we are doing things right. Use strong analytics to do this.

Roles

The world of predictive analytics is where I think the technical skills come back into play for those who are building the predictive modeling.

Let's make it clear that all skill levels have a place with the four levels of analytics, but the first two levels I would say are where those who are not technical data and analytics professionals, those who may be asked to utilize data in their roles, reside. The last two levels, predictive and prescriptive, are where the more technical reside.

We need to understand that all people have a role with all four levels of analytics, but it doesn't mean all have to have the same skill set. Data and analytics is not one-size-fits-all, not in the least. I want each of you reading this to know that you don't have to develop the same skills as another data and analytics professional. You don't need to develop the same skills I have within data and analytics—do you want to be that nerdy? Overall, you need to find where your skills gaps exist and then work towards filling those gaps. It is a continual process and one that I hope you will learn to love.

Within predictive analytics, the work that is done here can be of multiple folds and how one approaches it can be seen through the lens of that person's work, skills, and the need they have to use data. Let's explore different roles that exist within predictive analytics.

Leadership

Leadership is a big role within predictive analytics. Why might that be? The leadership are those who are guiding the future of a company, so predictions can be very important to them. I hope making smart, sound predictions is very, very important to them. We need leadership to make smart, well-informed predictions. Leadership should use a data-driven approach to predictions, where the prediction is a balance between the data and the human element. Let us remember that leadership may have vast experience and talent, strong thoughts and ideas, but we can't just leave it at that. We need leadership to develop those skills to utilize and read predictions well, combine them with their personal skills, and then make predictions.

Here we see one critical skill that leaders need to have in order to make or understand better predictions: the strong ability to read the data. Leaders need to be able to read data well. This could be reading the prediction as it has been built from the skills of data professionals or non-professionals. The leader needs to be able to internalize the data and information, compare and contrast it with other areas, and then use the information to make a decision on the prediction. This is one key thing: an executive may be reading a predictive analytic that has been built. This is great. Read it, understand what was built, and execute on it. An executive also may not have time for a full analysis or predictive analytic to be built, so instead they are reading descriptive analytics, combining it with their skill and experience, and then making a quick prediction. Time may not allow for the whole gambit of analytical work, so leaders need a good skill set to read the data, internalize it, combine it with their thoughts and experiences, and then make a predictive decision. Herein we see a skill set I may not have mentioned yet in the book and that is the ability to quickly internalize data and make a decision. This can be a powerful skill in a fast-paced environment. But we do need to develop it and not rest on our thoughts and experience.

Business or end user

The business or end user of data will primarily be working with predictive analytics from the standpoint of taking information from those building the predictions, reading it and understanding it, working with it, and then making predictions from the analytics. Now, here is a skill that the business or end user needs to have to work with predictive analytics: the ability to understand, read, and speak the language of predictive analytics.

Does this mean the person needs to be able to speak all the technical terms of predictive analytics? No, not at all. It does mean they need to be able to communicate effectively with those who are building the predictive analytics and they do need to develop a foundational level of knowledge around predictive analytics (and prescriptive analytics, but we will talk about that in Chapter 13). So, if you are a business or end user of data, develop a foundational knowledge of predictive analytics, learn some terms and terminology, network with those building the predictive analytics, and work together in a collaborative way to drive predictive analytics forward.

One key skill a business or end user can possess to help drive predictive analytics in an organization is the ability to ask good questions. Then, with the networking or relationship they have with those who build predictive analytics (if you don't have this network or relationship, build it), they can ask the question and let those data and analytics professionals get to work.

Data analyst

A data analyst is an interesting role within predictive analytics. Here, we see maybe a fusion or gray area. Some data analysts may be building predictive analytics, and some may not. If you are a data analyst who has not progressed or looked to progress to a data scientist role, but you have some skills and abilities, then please, build predictive analytics.

For some data analysts, it is like a business or end user of data. They will not necessarily be the technical person building the statistics or possibly advanced analytics, but they will be working with the results. The data analyst can also improve in asking questions so as to further the data and analytical work.

Data scientist

Here is a role that may be working a lot in predictive analytics, whether doing statistics or something else. Data scientists can be utilized within organizations to help drive predictive analytics.

A data scientist should bring their background and technical expertise in data and analytics to help an organization not only build predictive analytics but also communicate and teach on predictive analytics well. Data scientists are those who possess the skills to do deeper analysis, maybe even through statistics, to help drive insight and proper data and analytical work in an organization, but they potentially don't possess all the skills. Herein may be a skills gap needing to be filled: communication. Remember, a data scientist isn't just responsible for their work with data and analytics, and in this chapter in particular predictive analytics. No, they are also responsible for good communication around the predictive analytics itself. If

I haven't already mentioned in the book, the secret sauce of data and analytical work is the ability to communicate. If you see a need in yourself, if you are a data scientist or any role actually, or you see a need within your organization, help drive better communication. Build learning plans to help the organization succeed.

As a data scientist, you have a responsibility to build strong analytics for the organization. You may do this with statistics, building out statistical modeling to help you understand relationships within the data. You can build out statistics that you then utilize to help the organization make predictions. Predictive analytics can be a strong area for data scientists to work in within an organization.

Data engineer, machine learning engineer, and data architect (the backend of data roles)

For predictive analytics to work, we need good, sound data. In this case, we have the roles that encompass the backend of data. You can think of things as backend and frontend. Backend is the building of data and such, frontend is the analytics. Now, I understand these roles can help with frontend analytics, but I am simplifying and separating/delineating the roles here.

The backend team is tasked with building out the data. It needs to be built in a way that all four levels of analytics can take place. In our case with predictive analytics, the backend needs to ensure the modeling and cleanliness of the data is such that predictive analytics can be built. If we are dealing with garbage data on the backend, can we trust it in the frontend analytics? The adage of garbage in, garbage out can apply here. If we have bad data and make predictions from it, do we feel that this is going to be sufficient and work? Maybe if we are lucky. Instead, let's ensure the backend of data, the data quality, is strong, so that we can trust and feel good in our predictive analytics.

Tools and technologies

In the case of predictive analytics, we are getting more advanced in the technical skills that are needed. Not all tools will be technical *per se*. In fact, some of the tools can be the ones data analysts use, like coding with Python or R; it just may be that one is more advanced than the other. Coding is definitely a strong skill set to possess with predictive analytics.

Some tools that can be utilized here are Alteryx, SAP, and RapidMiner.[2] If you don't know what these tools are, a quick Google search can help people discover them or others. Data science isn't all about having to do all the coding and technical things anymore. Some tools you may find out there are designed to help simplify predictive analytics for people, like Alteryx. Rapidminer is another data science tool that doesn't require you to dig in all the way to the coding. Rapidminer is a no-code platform that allows the user to visualize the workflow.[3] Tools are becoming better at allowing end users to not be the most technical and still drive strong data science work.

This is one thing to keep in mind. Historically, the more advanced data and analytical work was being performed by those with more advanced skills. Now, tools and technology can simplify that for us. A word of caution though: don't just buy the shiny object because it says it will simplify things. Instead, invest in the right tool and technology that will hit your strategy. Think through the products, invest wisely, ensure proper and adequate training, and help to get adoption. Don't fall into the "shiny object" trap and buy a tool with the wrong purpose or intention. Study, learn, and use your organizational objectives to help you successfully pick the right tool and/or technology.

Chapter summary

Predictive analytics is a powerful part of analytics, when done appropriately. We don't want to just build predictive analytics for the sake of predictive analytics. Instead, we want to build targeted predictive analytics when we have utilized the descriptive analytics to understand the "what" and then diagnostic analytics for the "why." Now, we can start to build out some predictive analytics.

This can be exciting. Remember to have your predictive analytics in a process or system, where we possess the mindset that we know our prediction may be wrong, but we also know we will learn and iterate. In the next chapter, let us jump in and see how predictive analytics is used today.

CHAPTER DEFINITIONS AND TAKEAWAYS

- **Predictive analytics:** This is how it sounds: utilizing data and analytics to drive predictions. We want to predict things so we can then analyze those predictions and keep the gravy train rolling. We build a prediction and execute on that prediction, and then we can build descriptive and diagnostic analytics on the previous prediction and build new ones. What a wonderful cycle we are creating.

- **Predictive analytics and roles:** Each individual can have a role with predictive analytics but those roles will vary, of course. If you are a business or end user, you may just be utilizing the predictive analytic to understand things and what may be happening. You can then ask questions around the data and maybe drive more descriptive and diagnostic analytics. For data analysts, you also may not be building predictive analytics, but you may. Data scientists, you may be building these analytics. Data engineers, data architects, machine learning engineers (more involved in prescriptive analytics), you play a critical role with predictive analytics because we need good data to build good descriptive, diagnostic, and predictive analytics. Leadership, you need to understand the predictions, have a foundational knowledge of predictive analytics, and you need to have a keen eye to see how the predictions tie to the business strategy. If they don't, then scrap them and help drive better data-driven predictions.

Notes

1 Silver, N (2015) *The Signal and the Noise: Why so many predictions fail—but some don't*, Penguin Books

2 Scheiner, M (2020) 11 best predictive analytics tools (2022 Software Compared), *CRM.ORG*, https://crm.org/news/best-predictive-analytics-tools (archived at https://perma.cc/JAD4-V7M3)

3 Arnaldo, M, intro to Rapidminer: A no-code development platform for data mining, Analytics Vidhya, https://www.analyticsvidhya.com/blog/2021/10/intro-to-rapidminer-a-no-code-development-platform-for-data-mining-with-case-study/ (archived at https://perma.cc/M9A6-AHY4)

11

How are predictive analytics used today?

In this chapter, we will be building on the examples from chapters 5 and 8. This is a continuation of those examples, which helps us to see the story of the four levels of analytics and how they progress and work together. Hopefully, you will be able to glean ideas from these examples and see how this process operates. As you read through it, can you think of examples and ideas of where you can see the first levels of analytics at work? Can you see where in your personal and career lives you can improve in these areas? If you find areas for improvement, don't just find them, write down the gaps and create plans to improve in those areas. What good does it do us to study and learn about data and analytics, find gaps we have in our skills, and then not make plans to improve them? Write them down and build your plans for improvement. Let's jump into how predictive analytics are being used today.

Democratization of data—predictive analytics

The democratization of predictive analytics can be more interesting than the democratization of descriptive and diagnostic analytics. Those two levels of analytics are probably more universally democratized out, whereas predictive analytics may be democratized or we may see it more centralized in teams or areas of a business. Let me explain.

In the world of predictive analytics, we are dealing with more technical data and analytical work, so the democratization of this work looks a bit different. For the work itself, meaning the building, designing, modeling, etc., it may be concentrated in a small group of employees. It may be data scientists, data engineers, maybe some data analysts, who are doing the true data and analytical work to build the predictive analytics. Isolating the work to those professions is probably what we would call the opposite of democratization of data and analytics, of predictive analytics, but herein is where the beauty comes in from a truly data-literate and data-driven workforce. We don't democratize the work itself, we democratize the solutions, the predictions to the masses and allow them to work, allow their thoughts to grow and build.

One of my favorite quotes comes from the book *Snow Leopard* by Category Pirates and can be summarized as, the best kind of thinking we can do is to think about thinking. Another quote I like is by Albert Einstein: "If I had an hour to solve a problem, I'd spend 55 minutes thinking about the problem and five minutes thinking about solutions." Here is one way we can democratize predictive analytics. We send it to the masses or to the appropriate groups to help them "think" on the prediction and make decisions. This also illustrates a powerful part of the data and analytical train: the decision. Now, I will again recommend my friend's book, *Turning Data into Wisdom* by Kevin Hanegan, as this isn't a book on the data-driven decision-making process, but we need to think on these things so we know that when we democratize something like predictive analytics in an organization, we have the right end goal in mind. We need the end users and those who are receiving the predictions to have the ability to make a smart data-driven decision, not just receive the prediction and then go back to what they are comfortable with. That is not how this works if we are to do it properly.

Now, within the democratization of predictive analytics and to help drive a decision, does everyone in the company need to receive every single prediction? Expanding on that, does everyone even need to receive information on every decision that is made on predictions? Of course not, so don't think democratization of data means that everyone has to receive it. True democratization of data and analytics is giving everyone in an organization the ABILITY to receive or use data. It isn't that everyone will every time. The mindset, the culture, the data governance and data management structure are such that people can receive it when it is appropriate. Leadership must build a data and analytics strategy and culture that enables people to receive the right data at the right time. Your data and analytics strategy should be to support your business strategy. Some may think buying tools is a strategy. No, that is a part of the strategy. Make sure your strategy is to use data and analytics to achieve your business strategy.

Now, to expand on the *Snow Leopard* quote about thinking, I want to clarify that there are two ways to think of this. With regard to that quote, my boss at the time of writing this book, Derek Adams of BrainStorm, Inc., made a comment about a study showing adults versus children building a stack of marshmallows, something like that. In it, children go straight in building the marshmallow stack while adults decide on a plan or a solution. The kids do better. Both of these are good things. What matters is the context of the situation. In some cases, you have the time to think on the solution, to do as Einstein said, and in other instances what will matter is just getting going, just getting the ball rolling (another shout-out to Derek for that analogy from a work meeting we had). The reality is, we need to understand well the situation we are dealing with. This comes down to understanding the business and understanding the data train and what we are doing (data literacy). A great resource on business literacy with data is Jason Krantz.[1] By understanding the situation appropriately, we can then march forward with democratized predictive analytics in the correct manner. If you are just there to make a decision AND you are one who should be receiving the predictive analytics, then great, march forward and do your job. If you are one building the predictive modeling and analytics, great, understand who should and shouldn't have this information.

This does illustrate a key component to a data-driven culture: data fluency. The reality is, data fluency matters greatly. As the Godmother of Data Literacy, Valerie Logan, CEO and Founder of The Data Lodge, helps foster data literacy by intentionally treating it like a language, called Information as a Second Language® (ISL).[2] She believes we all can, and need to, speak the language of data to some degree—in both work and our personal lives. We need the frontend users to be able to communicate well (both speaking and listening) with those building the predictions and we need the backend people able to communicate well (both speaking and listening) with the frontend, explaining the prediction and what was built.

Democratization of predictive analytics—tools and technology

Here we come to the same discussion from the previous section of this chapter: tools and technology are not necessarily democratized, at least not those that are used to build the predictive analytics. Instead, it may be that the predictive analytics are used or overlayed in the tools that are democratized.

First, tools that require coding and other work to be done for the predictive analytics will or should be given to those who are building the predictive analytics. These tools and technologies are needed to help the individual build the predictive analytics. So, in this case, you may be talking about the more advanced tools or areas for coding languages that are used. The proper tools are necessary for the data and analytics professional to be able to build out the predictive analytics.

Now, what about how the predictive analytics are received by those who may just be business or end users of the analytics? In this case, you may see those tools used by these individuals, like Tableau or Excel, as democratized and utilized for the predictive analytics. One way the predictive analytics may be used by individuals is they are given the results and have to combine them with their work so that they can make smarter decisions.

So, once the predictive analytic is built, can it be used or overlayed with the descriptive and diagnostic analytics being used? Here, we can democratize the tools themselves, like Tableau, Qlik, or Excel, and then the users can use the information for their work. This is a way that predictive analytics tools and technologies, albeit it more advanced for people to build, are democratized through an organization. Again, strong data literacy skills and abilities are needed to properly utilize the predictive analytics in decision-making processes.

Data strategy and data governance

With us moving toward the more advanced analytical work, your data strategy and data governance program are important to your tool selection for the world of predictive analytics. Your tools should provide help toward your data strategy. Your data governance will help you decide who can have access to what data within a tool and maybe even who gets access to the tool. First, what is your data strategy? Do you know your own or your organization's? If not, please go and find it. If it doesn't exist, go and write it. Your data strategy, which will encompass your data governance program and strategy, will help guide you to what tools you need. Hopefully, it is clear how this works, but if not, let's examine it further.

DEFINE YOUR ORGANIZATION'S ROLES

Your strategy, whether it is vast and extensive, or small and you are just figuring things out, should show the use of data throughout your organization. Not just use, but who has access, what roles are in your organization, why those roles exist and what work they do. Please do not forget this, especially when you get to the more technical and advanced data and analytical workers. They have much talent and skill and we do not want them sitting on the sideline without clear direction or ideas. You should use your data strategy to specify what people will be doing. Now, it doesn't need to be so specific that they are micromanaged but it should be done in a way that allows the roles to understand what they are doing.

DECIDE HOW YOU WANT PREDICTIVE ANALYTICS TO WORK IN YOUR ORGANIZATION

Utilize your strategy to show how you want predictive analytics to be used. Don't just grab at straws or throw spaghetti or worse yet, just select things because they are buzz words or hyped up greatly. Instead, get specific on how you want predictive analytics to work in your organization. Then the roles and tools and technologies can present themselves and you will invest well.

USE YOUR TOOLS EFFECTIVELY

Now, the tools themselves. I won't go into specific tools or companies but this is something I would say: pick the tools that tie to the skill sets you have in the organization and that you are comfortable diving into and utilizing for the roles. Don't let the salesperson talk you into one because it is flashy, shiny, and they make it look great. Utilize smart, thought-driven decision making here. Test out multiple tools. Allow your data and analytics professionals to see them. Allow the professionals and yourself time to ask a lot of questions. With the end strategy and goal in mind, allow for the time to make the right decision. An example from my current work can help.

In my current role as I write this chapter, I have a data engineer working to build the right schema in place for us to succeed with a new product launch. That schema or backend work for our data strategy needs to be done in such a way that allows for the future development and work within all levels of analytics. We do have desires to utilize testing around the use of things. Of course we are looking at the famous and maybe the most widely used testing I know of: A/B testing. But I am big on Markov chain analysis. A/B testing, in brief, is testing a change to something against what is existent. Markov chain analysis is a fun way to predict where something will go next.[3] So, as my data engineer builds the backend architecture for our new product, it needs to be designed in a way that is strong, valid, and in a position to help build out the predictive modeling I want to see for the team and the organization. Then, when we are ready with the backend, we can choose the right tool and technology for us to run all predictive modeling that we may build. But note, we should always have in mind that we can be iterative with tools too, and guess what? If you find that tools aren't working the way you want, then cut and run to study a new tool. Don't keep a tool that doesn't really work for you and your organization. I think people need to be better at self-awareness; just because you have invested a lot of money in a tool and technology doesn't mean you should keep it in operation. No, iterate, find one that works better, and roll.

Data visualization, data storytelling, and more

We have spoken of data visualization and data storytelling as well as other areas as we march through the levels of analytics. I hope we are painting a strong picture of the holistic approach to analytical work and how it can flow through the four levels.

Data visualization

Data visualization can be a tool to help others understand the predictive analytics within your organization. Herein is a way that your more advanced data and analytical professionals work with other data and analytical professionals. What I mean here is if you have a data scientist who has run a strong predictive model, but you have data visualization specialists or data analysts who aren't able to run those advanced models, you have them work with the advanced data and analytical professional to build a data visualization around the prediction.

Now, let it be understood that not all predictions need to be built into a visualization, especially if you are running quick, one-off predictive analytics. Organizations should be using their data strategy and communication to help with one-off predictive analytics. When people know their roles and what is happening, it is easier to do analytics correctly. This is one great way that data literacy plays a crucial role in an organization. If people don't know what is happening, how data is being utilized to tie back to the business strategy, then it can go awry and not hit the goals you want. I don't want organizations to be frustrated in the work of predictive analytics and I don't want people siloed off. Having clear objectives and a clear, communicated strategy can help this.

Utilize the data visualization where appropriate with predictive analytics. In one role I held, we had the predictive analytic tied to a descriptive analytic for what was happening and it was built within a chart. You can do the same. Allow this to be a part of the data storytelling that you use as an organization to drive the knowledge around the predictive analytics being built in the organization.

Data storytelling

Communication may be the single most important factor in data and analytical work, and that means within predictive analytics. When one is building predictive analytics, it is imperative it is communicated well and intelligently through the organization. I just mentioned Markov chain analysis. How many people in your organization do you think know what that is? I can't go running around mentioning models and analyses that people haven't heard of. Change the wording of it to make sense to the masses. Ensure you are using proper data storytelling throughout the organization. I will speak to how to improve data storytelling in the next chapter.

For organizations today, data storytelling is a way of communicating out data and analytical work, but I am afraid it isn't utilized as powerfully as it should be. I would venture a guess that most organizations are not properly communicating out the predictive models that are being used. If you don't know in your organization, go and find out. Just take notes of how you see data being communicated throughout the organization. If you find gaps, then fill them. If you find it isn't being done well at all, be the star who brings it forward.

Coding

Coding will be a key area in how predictive analytics is being utilized in organizations. Those who are the advanced data and analytics professionals will be utilizing coding to help build the predictive analytics. Those who are not so advanced may use some coding, maybe to help build the data visualizations that carry the predictive analytic or maybe not. Finally, the end and business users probably won't be coding at all but receiving the work that was done by those who can code.

Statistics and probabilities

I hope this goes without saying, but for predictive analytics, individuals and organizations need to be using statistics and probabilities throughout the work. We can't build the diagnostic analytics, find the whys, and then stick our finger in the air and hope our guess gets us where we want to be. NO! Instead, utilize statistics and probabilities to help influence your predictive work. Don't just take what the data says. Bring the human element to the statistics and probabilities and drive the prediction forward. One of my favorite things is thinking. Think on the statistics and probabilities and then make decisions. Don't get caught in perfection or analysis paralysis but don't just jump to conclusions, either.

Industry examples—continued from Chapter 8

To conclude this chapter, let's keep our industry examples going and apply predictive analytics.

Healthcare

With the first two levels of analytics, descriptive and diagnostic, there was power to help drive smart decisions during the Covid-19 pandemic. When utilizing the data coming in and when dealing with an unknown, there were predictions made during the pandemic. Now, were these predictions always right? Of course not. Some may have been closer than others and yes, some could have been made with biases built in to suit a desired outcome (and no, we should not be using data and analytics to suit our needs. I hope I don't need to write on that, but please don't be subjective with your data and analytical work; be objective and use it to further goals, objectives, dreams, etc.). The key is to take in the information and iterate, make smarter data-driven predictions, and go. We should be taking in data around the health crisis and driving forward to make intelligent decisions.

One example we have been using is that of hospital beds. As you can imagine, predicting capacity of hospital beds is vitally important. There is a children's hospital relatively close to where I live that has recently shut down elective surgeries because of the illnesses going around. The beds are full or filling up and I hope they are using predictive modeling in some way to understand the needs of the rooms and making the decision to not have elective surgeries. Predictive modeling in healthcare is vitally important.

Retail

As I write this chapter, the holiday shopping season is upon us. It is important during this season that retail organizations know how much inventory to have. Using the modeling, organizations should be able to utilize predictive analytics in a powerful way to drive how much stock to keep and how to make decisions on the shoppers.

With the employee example I mentioned, for organizations looking to ramp up hiring or bring in seasonal workers for the holiday season, doing this by "best guess" methodology may work but may not. Instead of just guessing and then having too many people on staff and not enough work, organizations can utilize predictive power to bring people in when needed. That said, retail organizations need to be smart about this and iterate as they may find the model predicted too many or too few. See, here I go again with the iterative mindset. We need to have that as part of our mindset with data and analytical work.

Marketing

What company that you know of goes into a marketing campaign and says, "you know, I hope we don't get more customers" or whatever the campaign is for? Well, guess what, no, that's not what they say. Whether it is to drive new customers, sell existing customers on a new product, or build the brand, marketing wants success. Strong predictive modeling and analytics is one way for this to occur.

Utilizing predictive analytics, along with descriptive and diagnostic analytics, organizations can utilize marketing toward its customer base. Using these things in an ethical, appropriate manner, organizations can utilize predictive analytics to see and predict how certain things will operate with its customer or non-customer base. Predictive analytics isn't a perfect crystal ball but hopefully, marketing is using it in such a way that the crystal ball is helping to shape how they want things to be done.

Finance, financial services, and banking

I don't think these industries use predictive analytics at all… I am kidding. I sure hope they are using it extensively! Think about it: when a bank issues you a loan for something substantial, they are going to want to know of your ability to pay it back. Does this mean that predictive modeling is perfect? No, of course not and in fact, it has messed up in financial industries by denying loans, but the black box algorithm may have been poor.

In one role at American Express, I inherited predictive modeling on write-off rates and delinquencies. This matters greatly! Understanding how much may be written off can help a bank or financial services company know how much money to hold in reserve. The predictions that were set around the 2008 housing and financial crisis were either junk or not taken seriously enough by enough people. Here we need to realize that predictions can't just be made and ignored. If we want to be the most successful we can be, predictions are good, but maybe more important is how we use them and how we learn from them.

Supply chain and logistics

Predictive modeling within supply chain and logistics can be vitally important. With the Covid-19 pandemic, there was a supply chain issue. Having a solid understanding of what is happening (descriptive analytics) and why it is happening (diagnostic analytics), can be key to helping build predictions about it. If there is a supply chain crisis, knowing what to do next could be the key to help solve the crisis. It may be a few steps down the road, but one prediction today could lead to another and another. Then, we have utilized the first three levels to help us out of the crisis.

Data ethics and predictive analytics

Like descriptive and diagnostic analytics, a key area to be careful with within predictive analytics is the ethical use of predictions; it is vital in predictive analytics to not be discriminatory. We need to ensure that we are building predictive analytics objectively and with an ethical mindset. Data and analytics should be objective, not full of bias. Now, one may say that if we use machines to do this, the codes and machines may be built by a human. That is true, so we need to ensure we have strong data literacy that allows us to understand the data objectively and to question it appropriately.

Another area of data and analytics that taps into predictive analytics and ethics is our personal bias. Like with descriptive and diagnostic analytics, are we objectively looking at the data or are we seeking answers? If we are looking for answers that conform to our beliefs, then we aren't looking at it objectively. Let's ensure we are objectively looking at the predictive analytics and we are using those predictions appropriately.

Chapter summary

Predictive analytics is what it says it is. We are predicting things. But, we should have a solid use of descriptive and diagnostic analytics to help us drive strong predictions. Predictions are used a lot today. Does that mean they are good predictions? Of course not! We need a strong, holistic approach to all the levels of analytics to make the solid predictions that will carry us forward to drive better outcomes.

CHAPTER DEFINITIONS AND TAKEAWAYS

- **Democratization of predictive analytics:** The democratization of predictive analytics is an interesting one. Is everyone going to build these analytics? No! But appropriate parties need to know about them, especially if it involves their roles or business units. Predictions themselves can be democratized, the information, but the work won't necessarily be democratized. Predictive analytics is more advanced and will sit with more advanced data and analytics professionals.

- **Predictive analytics in data strategy:** We need to remember to not get ahead of ourselves with predictive analytics. Descriptive analytics is where companies are stuck and predictive and prescriptive are where companies spend a lot of money as they are the exciting levels. Diagnostic analytics is the one left behind. Within a data strategy, predictive analytics needs to be utilized correctly. Build good predictions with the data after sound understanding and knowledge is obtained with descriptive and diagnostic analytics. Ensure your predictions also tie to business goals and objectives. We could build some really cool predictions but what if they don't tie to anything? Well, that could be really bad.

Notes

1 https://www.linkedin.com/in/jasonkrantz/
2 The Data Lodge: https://www.thedatalodge.com/ (archived at https://perma.cc/5UC7-5KKY)
3 To find out more about Markov chains, see https://www.upgrad.com/blog/markov-chains/ (archived at https://perma.cc/QB7E-WAHX)

12

How individuals and organizations can improve in predictive analytics

We have taken the time to talk about what predictive analytics is and how predictive analytics is being used, now let's jump into a baby of mine: how individuals and organizations can improve in predictive analytics. Improvement in predictive analytics will span across both the technical and the non-technical. Let's start with the non-technical.

Data and analytics mindset—predictive analytics

The right mindset is critical to predictive analytics. Do predictions always come true? Of course not! But that doesn't mean everyone has that mindset. Some examples of where the mindsets differ and how we approach and deal with predictions can help us to understand the mindset we need with predictive analytics.

One example I use when I speak deals with an election within the United States. Now, I won't talk politics in this, no, but the election shows a good example of the wrong mindset (not to mention the poor design of the predictions that were out there). The 2016 presidential election is a wonderful case study for predictions and what not to do, mindset-wise.

With the 2016 presidential election, the predictions were leaning toward Hillary Clinton and in some cases they were leaning heavily toward her. As the election occurred, I think some thought it was in the bag. But here is the thing: there are two sides to a prediction. What I mean by this is if something, anything, is predicted to have a 70 percent chance of happening, that means 7 out of 10 times it will happen and 3 out of 10 times it won't, or 30 out of 100 times, or 300 out of 1,000 times, or 30,000 out of 100,000 times... and you get the point. Seventy percent is a high likelihood but in 3 out of 10 elections, Hillary Clinton was not going to win. I believe there was at least one prediction that was higher than 70 percent. Now, we are not going to talk about anything else with the election apart from the predictions and the mindset towards them (and we can speak about the way the predictions were built later, if at all). How did people react to the outcome of the election?

Some people were not happy at all! This is the wrong mindset and I am not talking about whether you were happy with the election or not. No, I am talking about the mindset to have so much confidence that the prediction is what will happen. I am not saying you can't have confidence, no, but I am saying we can all probably improve our mindset toward the understanding that predictions aren't perfect science. We don't know perfectly. Instead, we develop the right mindset, the iterative mindset. The mindset matters. Looking at predictions and knowing ok, even with 95 percent chance of something happening, that means 5 out of 100 times it won't go the way we think it will. That isn't a whole ton, but it is something. We have to have the right mindset for predictions and this is one way we can improve in predictive analytics. Let's look at another example: sports.

The mindset matters

How often do we cheer for the underdog? It is something that happens often. But let me ask you this: what does being an underdog mean? It means you aren't the one who is supposed to win (i.e. the prediction is not leaning your way. That said, we expect it to happen; upsets can be fun). We have the mindset that it *can* happen. But, with elections, we may not tell ourselves that it can happen. We can see the differences between these two things. This is an improvement we need to have so let's talk on it more.

What is it that makes us like underdogs or expect these things to happen? One thing may be that we are accustomed to seeing these things happen. So, how do we develop our mindset to be open as we are with underdogs if we aren't used to it happening? First, we need to develop an open data and analytical mindset, which means we develop the understanding that outcomes, although they may be likely, may not occur. This is something we can tell ourselves and prep ourselves for the outcomes that may be. Herein is another way to develop this mindset.

We can develop an ability to look at possible outcomes: those that hit the prediction, those that don't, and those that may partially hit the prediction. By looking at possible outcomes and their impact, we can develop a talent and ability to see the other sides. This can help us to deal with impact, outcomes, and iterate and move through things.

Now, the mindset above is really focused on individuals; how can organizations utilize this type of mindset or improve in it? First, the learning opportunities, the data literacy piece of this, are vital. So, an organization can provide the right learning opportunities. I won't expand much on the learning opportunities as far as taking courses at this point, but know that learning opportunities need to be there. But how can we develop learning opportunities here or how can we permeate them through the organization? Proper communication is vital for this. As organizations build predictions, share them out, and make decisions on them, then the communication of how the prediction is built, how the decision is made, and possible outcomes, is vital. When building predictions:

- there needs to be trust that it was built well;
- there needs to be understanding of what the decision is and who is executing on the decision;
- finally, there needs to be communication around all of this and the possible outcomes.

These are things organizations can do to improve mindset.

Another way the mindset can be built into predictive analytics in the organization is a clear-cut part of the data and analytics strategy that shapes the iterative approach to data and analytical work, especially with regard to predictions. Predictions aren't perfect and the holistic approach to data and analytical work—where we are ongoing and we are learning, growing, utilizing descriptive and diagnostic analytics over and over—is how we need to approach predictive analytics.

Finally, we can speak of one of my favorite things within data and analytics (plus one of my 3 C's of data literacy): curiosity. As predictions are being built, how comfortable are the data and analytics professionals if people come by and question, in a good manner, what they are doing? If they could approach it a different way? This is an aspect of a mindset with regard to communicating and doing data and analytical work: we are comfortable with our work but are we comfortable with people questioning our work?

Another way to question predictive analytics is that when we see the outcome, we can question what happened, why it happened, what caused it to happen, and we can develop the mindset that we may be wrong but we can work toward continual improvement.

Predictive analytics and the tridata

I mentioned this before, but there are books on doing statistics and building predictions. I am not going to build out the technical side in this book, but instead let's dive into predictive analytics and data-driven problem solving, data-driven decision making, and data-driven execution. Let's start with data-driven problem solving within predictive analytics.

Predictive analytics and data-driven problem solving

How can we improve in our predictive analytics and data-driven problem solving? One key area where we can do this is in our ability to look at predictions, what we are predicting, and the problem we are looking at specifically. Get really good at thinking on the data and the problem you are solving, really understand how the problem ties back to the organization's goals, and understand how the prediction helps with the problem itself. This is an interesting one. Does this require technical skills? I don't think it does. Can technical skills help here? Yes, they can help us do things, but what I want you to think on is how well do I think on the data? How well do I meditate on and ponder the outcome and the problem? Now, you may say to yourself, I don't have time for that. Yes, you do! I get that most, if not everyone, has or says they have a busy job. That is ok. You can find the time. There is probably a lot of work we don't need to do, plus the thinking and pondering work may pay greater dividends than busy work. The reality is, busy work isn't necessarily effective work. We need to focus on truly effective work that helps move the needle forward for our organizations.

As an individual, you can get really good at understanding the problem and how you are approaching it, then really improving your ability to work with the data and analytics professionals to communicate the needs and wants of a prediction. If you are the individual building the prediction, your role is understanding how the problem is being solved and the business outcomes of the organization, and your job is to get good at listening to those communicating the need to you and then bouncing questions back off of them. This will allow you to build out stronger predictions that can help with the problem solving. Data and analytics professionals and non-professionals working together in tandem and understanding possible outcomes can help drive the best data-driven problem solving there can be.

An example, going back to our election, can help us understand data-driven problem solving and how we can improve in predictive analytics. One way we can improve in our predictive analytics and data-driven problem solving is to have retrospectives. When we are looking at predictions, taking a step back and comparing the predictive analytics to the outcome can allow us to dissect down the outcome and the prediction and maybe more importantly how we built the prediction. By understanding how a prediction is built, we can dig in and apply our problem solving and work with the prediction.

With the 2016 US presidential election, we can look at how the predictions were built (let's face it, some were built poorly) and then apply a better way of looking at things for future predictions, in this case, future elections. We need to understand what problem we were solving and then how the predictions worked for better or worse. Then, maybe our learnings will teach us both how to do better data-driven problem solving and how we can improve our predictions.

Remember those rules I used with diagnostic analytics? Let's continue them here with data-driven problem solving and predictive analytics:

1 Set a rule that with the proposed solutions you have, you have a good understanding of them and build at least one prediction per solution. Allow this to help you build a lineage or train from the outcome to the problem solving to the solutions to the predictions of the solutions. See how this all works together? What we want is to know what the business outcome is. We then want to understand the descriptive analytics around the outcome. Then, with the diagnostic analytics built out, we can then think of proposed solutions. With each of the proposed solutions in place, we then build a prediction from each. Then, monitor them.

2 This is not the same number 2 as in Chapter 9—that will be number 3 in this chapter. Number 2 is to build a good monitoring and reviewing process. You need to monitor how things are going. You can be building descriptive and diagnostic analytics as they go. But, have a review process in place to ensure your building is strong and you can learn and iterate. Does it make sense to build out a prediction that you don't monitor? Of course not.

3 Again, enlist the help of others. You need to have the right voices at the right table for the predictive analytics you are building out. As you monitor how it is all going, do not isolate just yourself into an echo chamber of understanding how things are performing. Enlist others, learn from them, and understand what is going on. Others can have different perspectives and may be able to dig into

problems more and more. Hopefully, we can see good, strong perspectives to different pieces.

4 I am going to echo my rule for diagnostic analytics: if you can't think of how to predict things or if you are struggling to understand the predictions that have come through, go for a walk. Allow yourself some time away and truly bring out your thinking power for success. Yes, we live in a fast-paced world and we have busy jobs, but I think just adding a bit more thinking can be powerful. If you haven't heard of my daily 15 rule, you need to. There are 1,440 minutes in a day. One percent of your day is 14.4 minutes, let's round that up to 15. Mark down a daily 15: 15 minutes a day to think on the data and analytics in front of you. If it is working with predictive analytics, then great, think on predictive analytics. If it is diagnostic, then great, think on diagnostic analytics. You need to give yourself time to think on the data and work, and you need it to drive forward.

5 If you are struggling with how to predict things or understand the predictive analytics that have been given to you, I want you to journal and write things down. Start to write down your thoughts and ideas. It doesn't have to be anything big or scientific. If you are stuck and not sure what to do, just start doing something. Have you heard of the phrase "throw spaghetti on the wall and see what sticks"? Throw different ideas out or start to write your theories down. Just start writing, start working, start thinking.

With diagnostic analytics, we started to discuss that ideation is not the end goal, but that you then need to dig in. Let's follow those steps with predictive analytics:

- First, gather the data or ideas that you need. With the prediction, you hopefully have the data already that allowed the diagnostic analytics to be formed. Then, I want you to start thinking about the data and what you need to do to build the predictive analytics. It may be just communicating with the right people or it may be that you will be the one building the predictive analytics. But, you need to have the right ideas, people, and data in place to succeed.

- Build your predictive analytics (it was build your data visualization with diagnostic analytics in Chapter 9). Again, this may take a couple of forms. It may be that you need to work with those who build predictive analytics first or it may be that you are building it. But the key is to do what needs to be done or as my boss, Derek Adams, CTO of BrainStorm, inc. says, get the ball rolling.

So, we have seen how predictive analytics plays a part in problem solving. Hopefully, we are seeing how it can play a direct part within problem solving as we are building predictions and it can help us to see if our solutions were correct. The predictions can help us see if our diagnostic analytics were correct. Let's move on to data-driven decision making.

Predictive analytics and data-driven decision making

Predictive analytics is a way to confirm and work with data-driven decision making to show the possible outcomes of what may happen with our decisions. This is amazing and may be crucial. Think about it. If we are proposing solutions, wouldn't it be nice to see what possible outcomes are? Also, predictive analytics can lead us to understand the diagnostic analytic that helps us understand what is happening.

First, let's look at the possible outcomes. If we are making decisions with data, we can look to build some predictive analytics around the different scenarios so we can understand the likelihood of things happening. This is power. If we have come to four possible diagnostic analytics, then we use those to make decisions and utilize the power of predictive analytics to understand what could happen. This opportunity to see what could happen is power. What if you feel you have landed on the pot of gold at the end of the rainbow? If you think you have landed at this great diagnostic analytic and then build predictions on what will happen with the outcomes of those decisions, what if they turn things sour and don't look great? What a great tool.

One thing I love with data and analytics is looking at unintended consequences. Use this with predictions: What things could we possibility not be looking at? Is there anything? What could possibly happen that leads to poor outcomes? Use predictions intelligently and wisely with your decisions.

Second, predictive analytics can be a tool to help us understand the correct diagnostic analytic. We can build descriptive analytics and utilize predictive analytics that show what possible diagnostic analytics could be there. This is where it isn't working in a linear fashion within the four levels of analytics. We have the descriptive analytics and we can use predictive analytics to help predict the diagnostic analytic. Then, we can use predictive analytics to show the possible outcomes of the newly discovered diagnostic analytics, found through predictive analytics. Confused yet? I hope not. I hope this illustrates the power of analytics to do things and make decisions.

Predictive analytics and data-driven execution

This becomes more simple: you will have built or had built for you the predictive analytics, now I want you to be a leader and help the decision get executed upon. Be vocal, be communicative, and help drive the execution of decisions. It isn't going to be any good for you or the organization to build awesome descriptive analytics, awesome diagnostic analytics, and awesome predictive analytics, only to have it fall flat.

Lead the groups, lead the decisions, work with the teams, ensure execution and help where you can. Then, monitor the solutions appropriately. If you are building the predictive analytics, use your skills and abilities to help build the descriptive analytics as you go. Help drive diagnostic analytics, either through ideation or using predictive modeling to help build those predictive analytics. It isn't that you need to just sit back and wait to drive iteration and utilizing the train over and over again. You can be iterating as you go. Use it and roll with it! I like this part a lot. I like iteration. I like the power behind all we have been talking about. Let's do this appropriately, not sitting back and waiting but working forward over and over again. This is power and this is what we can do.

Chapter summary

Predictive analytics is powerful and fun. We have discussed the tridata and how predictive analytics fits within it. I may have said this already in the book, but the key is knowing where you fit in. Find your place with predictive analytics, whether in your personal life, as the skills translate there, or in your organization. I hope you are seeing how you fit in and that you have a place at the table. A quick personal story can hopefully bring to life for you how this can work. I hope this can spark an idea either in your personal or career life on how to use predictive analytics.

Remember my Speedgoat race? I can use the descriptive analytics and diagnostic analytics to understand my Speedgoat 50k race, but then I need to build some predictions. How should I fuel? How should I hydrate? What can I do? I can build some predictions for that race or any other I may do. That can help me prep well and be smart, but let's not just iterate once or at the end. As I train for a race, I could in theory make predictions every day on what to do and outcomes. Then, I can learn from them, make decisions, learn from them, make decisions. That is iteration. That is the mindset I need to have, ongoing and working well. It's time for all of us to roll with the four levels of analytics.

We have now finished the first three levels—let's jump into level 4.

CHAPTER DEFINITIONS AND TAKEAWAYS

- **Predictive analytics and mindset:** We have probably spoken about this with mindset already, but let's tie it back to how we can have the right mindset with predictions. Do we think that every prediction is going to come to pass? I hope not! Predictions are just that, predictions. They aren't prophecy or revelations that are bound to happen, so when they don't, we should not be freaking out. Instead, understand that we can learn from the prediction and keep going.

- **Predictive analytics and the tridata:** Each level of the tridata is powerful but here, predictions really deal with decision making and execution. We need to utilize predictive analytics to help drive what our decision will be and then we need to execute on that decision. Don't just build powerful predictions and then go on your merry way, doing things as you always have. Utilize the predictive analytic combined with your human element, meaning your ideas, thoughts, gut feel, experience, and make decisions and then execute on those decisions.

13

Prescriptive analytics

What are prescriptive analytics?

Do you hear that noise? Listen carefully. Do you hear the robot coming back from the future to prevent things from happening? Do you hear the sound of robots marching outside, coming to prevent you from leaving your house so they can take over all the jobs? Let's start to chat about prescriptive analytics and no, this is not how it is going to happen.

Referencing back to our diagram of the four levels of analytics, Figure 4.1, we are in that final stage. Here, we have potentially the most helpful technology for us as humans within data and analytics, if it is built and done right, and we also have what may be the level that requires the most technical skills to build out the prescriptive analytics. Prescriptive analytics is where something external, in this case the machine, tells us what we should be doing.

A couple of definitions can help here. One definition from Talend tells us that prescriptive analytics is where technology is used on data to help us understand trends that exist and then to make instant recommendations on the predicted outcomes.[1] Pretty straightforward. The machines will dig through our data, using technology like machine learning to dig through the data, find trends and patterns, and then make recommendations. Now, this helps lead to how people are using prescriptive analytics, which we will talk about in the next chapter.

> Hint: We need sound data literacy to know how to interact with the machine that is providing us with the prescriptive analytics.

Another definition of prescriptive analytics comes from the website techtarget.com and it says that prescriptive analytics is the type of analytics that tells us what should happen next.[2] Think about that: the technology, utilizing the data, drives for us what should happen next. Think of it like a crystal ball. Now, does this mean it will be perfect and we should automatically just utilize what this "crystal ball" of analytics tells us? NO! First, the technology will not be perfect. Second, we need to apply the human element. We may not have the computing power of technology, but technology does not have the human element built in. We want to have a combination of the two: the data and the human. To help us understand prescriptive analytics more, let's dive back into two examples: the doctor's visit (you aren't going back to doctors that want to give you just a descriptive analytic and leave, right?) and my racing example with the Speedgoat 50k.

The doctor example is quite easy to utilize here because we sometimes get prescriptions. What exactly is a prescription? Let's look at it the way I explain it to tie back to prescriptive analytics. A prescription is an external thing that we take to improve us. So, we take a pill or medication that is there to help us to get better, an external thing to help improve our situation. Think of this as it ties back to data and analytics. An external thing, like machine learning or like an algorithm, like Talend mentions, is there, utilizing the organization's data to tell us what we should do. That is amazing! So, an external thing, like a doctor giving us a medication, is there to help us improve. Now, this doesn't mean that is all that needs to be done. When we are sick, we may have this medication, but we may require other things to help us get better. Maybe the medication is there to help us with pain after a surgery, but, depending on the surgery, we may be going through physical therapy. Also, when it comes to this type of surgery, we may not be able to just jump back into things like we have done before. I love fitness and have had back, elbow, and hernia surgeries in the past. I couldn't just go right back to what I was doing the next day; I had to get back to it gradually. The same thing can be said with machine learning to the extent that we can't just jump into the machine learning recommendation and role. There may be steps we take afterward to make the smartest decision.

With the Speedgoat 50k race, we saw the descriptive analytic showing me just how much sweat I had lost (over 23 pounds, and that is still crazy to think about). With that descriptive analytic, how could prescriptive analytics help me in my prep for another race? Now, I wish I had this set up, maybe something I need to take on. But imagine I fed all my workout data into a program that spit out and showed me exactly what I needed to do: the amount of food I needed to eat, the amount of water to consume, and not just on race day, but daily. Imagine if it told me I needed to train this much and sleep this much. That would be cool science, but guess what, I don't necessarily want that. Why, you may ask? Because I like having the freedom to work out how I want to work out, to do the things I enjoy. That said, if I am to run another ultra (and at the writing of this book, I am gaining more desire to do another), I will need to commit and put in the work. But I like the flexibility of working out how I want. Herein we have the data and the human element combining. If one day I am recommended to run xx miles and I feel more like riding my spin bike, well, I am going to hop on my exercise bike and spin. Then, I can input the data into the program and it will recalculate and move forward. The prescriptive analytic I would like is one that spits out a variety of programs and ideas and then I take the time and assess, see how I am feeling, and jump in.

It isn't just the working out though. What if it was telling me to stretch xx amount of time, meditate, what I should eat, etc. Just like if I wasn't feeling a certain thing on a certain day, I have the ability to modify and select what I want, put the new information into the program (machine learning) and it learns, progresses. This is an element of machine learning: the more data it gets, the more information, the more it can learn, and the more it can improve (thank you to a person I met with at Seek.AI who shared how their machine learning or AI can work, which I am extrapolating here). In essence, if·I input more and more information into my machine learning algorithm, my hope is that it will learn, improve, and get better at spitting out those "what we should do" recommendations.

Now, I don't want to lose sight of this combination of the data and the human element working together. We must never lose sight of it. If you don't feel like working out a certain way but it tells you to? Well, maybe you shouldn't that day. The reality is, we have inputs that the machine might not have; maybe in the future it can help, but what if it is recommending a punishing workout but your job is weighing on you and you feel exhausted? If the machine doesn't take that into consideration you may be punishing yourself too much and absolutely hindering your health. So, ensure you are bringing that human element and the data element together to make smart decisions.

Let's turn back to the examples we utilized in descriptive analytics to show what prescriptive analytics is. To start, let's turn back to write-off and delinquency rates.

Write-off and delinquency rates

In my role at American Express I was responsible for building the descriptive and predictive analytics for the write-off and delinquency rates for the portfolios I was responsible for. That is the human element building the write-off and delinquency rates. Now, maybe someone likes to think themselves perfect or that their way of doing things is the perfect way of doing things, but that is not me. Sure, we all have parts of us that like to think our way is the way and yes, we may become resistant to people challenging us (shame on us if they are challenging us in an appropriate manner—that is how we can grow and improve). But the reality is we are human. Now, imagine if a machine or algorithm was building the write-off and delinquency rates for us, and not only doing that but telling us what our next step would be with those rates. Now, do not be mistaken: machines are not perfect! Also remember, that sometimes the data we are feeding the machine is prepared by a human, giving another opportunity for human error to enter the picture. But the machine can take the time to learn and then improve on the information that is presented within it.

Let's face it, computers have much greater capacity than us to calculate and process things. They can do many things while we may still be processing one thing. This is fact. Again, this does not mean that the computer is perfect. No, not at all. Tools and technologies have issues, but we can harness their power to process and calculate things for us. Then, we can utilize those things and make decisions. Remember, the machine learning or algorithm will tell us what to do, but it is up to us to harness the data and technology element and combine it with the human element.

With the write-off and delinquency rates, I can imagine the power of machine learning to run hypothetical scenarios, to calculate the data I needed quickly, giving me my time back. Also, I can imagine that if I were to have used machine learning, different scenarios or options could have been populated for us. We wouldn't have just had descriptive and predictive analytics at our fingertips; imagine if the prescriptive analytics gave us five different possible scenarios and then told us what to do to drive home results. During a chaotic time such as after the housing crash, having options, utilizing the comput-ing power of technology, could have empowered us so much more than utilizing just little old me to build the analytics. Having machine learning or algorithms building things for me and then offering suggestions for what to do? Yes, that would have been amazing and fun. Now, I would have needed the skills to interact with and utilize the things the prescriptive analytics were spitting out to me, but I will talk about that more in the roles section.

Monthly average users

In my current role, as I build out the backend data architecture that will empower us to do the frontend analytics, I would love to have prescriptive analytics flowing through the work and offering up suggestions of what to do.

Technology companies want their software to be adopted. Imagine if I had machine learning built into my work where not only was the algorithm or technology studying the data and average users, but also studying the average users in the machine and helping build out what they were doing with our technology or with the technology of those organizations we have partnered with. Wouldn't that be amazing? Yes, it would! This is the advancement I want to see companies take on. There is absolutely power in the descriptive and diagnostic analytics that people in organizations build. In fact, with the proper democratization of data through an organization, having multiple eyes and hands bring their human element to the data and analytics table is power. But what I also want to see is the combination of that power with the power of prescriptive analytics and technology. For my case here, I would love to direct some machine learning at the users of our software and the software of our partners. That machine learning can work toward understanding more and more of the user base. We can dig into the behavior of the users and use it to make more targeted assignments or things the users can do. Instead of sticking my finger in the air and taking guesses, we are now working toward targeted triggers. Those triggers can then be utilized to empower better software adoption and behavior change.

Not only can we send more targeted triggers to the users themselves, but I can use machine learning to help us understand what kind of assets to build for the end users. So, not only are we sending them targeted things, but I can use the prescriptive analytics to tell me what to be building.

Note, and this is a big note: we don't always have to do what the machine tells us. Remember, we don't want to eliminate the human element. So, combine your skills and knowledge with the technology and then make decisions.

Decision making

I am going to keep this a general category. Do you ever find yourself stuck on a decision and don't know what to do? My wife and I can get stuck on where to eat dinner, which would seem like a simple decision. Now, magnify that out to decisions in business that can be difficult:

- Do we need to downsize the company?
- Should we go on a hiring spree?
- Should we launch a new product, or should we enhance existing products?
- Are our customers happy and satisfied with our current offerings or should we do something that could help them smile more?

These can be tough decisions, especially those that deal with people. It can be hard, but machines can help. That said, in no way am I advocating that we take the human element out and let a "cold box" tell us what to do, no. I am suggesting that in the decision-making process, we can utilize the computational power of technology to build out some prescriptive analytics for us. With those prescriptive analytics, we can be better armed with more information to make a better data-driven decision. Within decision making, the power of the technology can be paramount. Maybe in some cases we are so stuck that yes, we just use the machine to drive the decision, but please in some way utilize the human element in that. Also, remember that the machine or algorithm may have been built by humans, who are not perfect (sorry to say that, but we are inherently flawed). We might not be perfect but we are powerful! Utilize that power, YOUR power, with prescriptive analytics.

Roles

Roles for prescriptive analytics are unique and awesome. The actual building of the technologies or the use thereof for those things outside of the prescriptions themselves is going to be owned by potentially quite a few. How many people do you know who could write and code an algorithm? How many people do you know who could help build out the machine learning in your organization; who would have the knowledge and skill to do so? If you don't know anyone who could do that, hey, guess what, these roles pay nicely so maybe you can jump in and start to become one. I am just saying.

The reality is, the actual technical skills for these roles are going to be owned by few. If you are looking to find a niche and don't know where to go in your journey within data and analytics, and this area excites you, then maybe you could look into the skills necessary for prescriptive analytics. I would love to hire a machine learning engineer or someone who can build powerful algorithms. If I can find a good one, I may have struck gold within my team in building out data and analytics for my company. So, if their skill is possessed by few, what are the roles that deal with these skills?

The reality is the skill we need for prescriptive analytics if we are not building them is to have the ability to deal with the outcomes the prescriptive analytical tools and technologies give us. Do you have that skill? Do you have the ability to take what the technology is sending you and to make combined human and data-driven decisions? In steps the powerful and wonderful world of data literacy.

Remember, we aren't needing to turn all of us into machine learning engineers, AI-building scientists, or powerful coders building powerful algorithms. The actual number of people in an organization who will be doing those things is small. What shouldn't be small is our ability to interact with the technology and what it is telling us.

Within an organization, this can be every single role. If you are an executive or in the C-suite, your role may be to take the prescriptive analytic and drive a decision home with it, combining it with your skills. If you are a data analyst, your role may be to combine the prescriptive analytic with the descriptive, diagnostic, and predictive, to build a powerful data story and drive it home to the audience. If you are a data scientist or engineer, you may be tweaking the codes and algorithms or monitoring the machine learning and adjusting as needed. As a business or end user, you may be taking the results and combining them with your decision-making process. Everyone can have a role with prescriptive analytics, even though it is an advanced and technical field within data and analytics. Isn't that powerful, knowing you have a seat at this table? I hope you realize you do!

Tools and technologies

With prescriptive analytics being mainly driven by technology, I will save the discussion on tools and technologies for the next chapter on how prescriptive analytics is being used in the world today.

Chapter summary

Prescriptive analytics is like the prescription drug you are given to help you get better. It is an external thing telling you what you need to do; like a prescription helps fix you when you are sick, a prescriptive analytic is going to tell you what to do to achieve the greatest outcome. That said, it doesn't mean we are forgetting us, the human element. Just like we can't take a prescription and just think things will be better, we need to not just take the prescriptive analytic and run with it. We need the human element to play a crucial role. This means you and everyone you know have seats at this table.

CHAPTER DEFINITIONS AND TAKEAWAYS

- **Prescriptive analytics:** Think of this as the technical, robots taking over level. No, I don't think we are going to have a robot uprising on our hands, not at all. But here we have an analytical level that is there to supplement us. Utilize machine learning and technologies to help make decisions. This is a powerful level of analytics because it can simplify our lives, especially with mundane tasks.

- **Machine learning and artificial intelligence:** These are advanced technologies at our disposal. Think of machine learning as machines learning, utilizing the data, and then spitting out recommendations to us. Now, we want to combine these recommendations with our human element to help make decisions.

- **Roles:** Now, we aren't looking at many people *building* prescriptive analytics, as those will be the advanced data and analytics professionals. Instead, we will have a larger group that *uses* these analytics.

Notes

1 Talend (nd) What is prescriptive analytics? https://www.talend.com/resources/what-is-prescriptive-analytics/ (archived at https://perma.cc/9T3W-T7U2)

2 Lawton, G (nd) Prescriptive analytics, *TechTarget*, https://www.techtarget.com/searchcio/definition/Prescriptive-analytics (archived at https://perma.cc/9JEH-VEHP)

14

How are prescriptive analytics used today?

I hope you now have an understanding of what prescriptive analytics is. I also hope you aren't running for the hills thinking robots are taking over, nor do I want you thinking you need to develop all the technical skills possible that will allow you to build or code within prescriptive analytics. No, I want you to find that you fit within prescriptive analytics and maybe you need some more skills, but you don't need to be the advanced data and analytics professional.

In this chapter, we are going to dive into how prescriptive analytics is or can be used in the world today. Let's start off with how predictive analytics is used today and the democratization of prescriptive analytics.

Democratization of data—prescriptive analytics

To be honest, I am not sure how many companies are democratizing prescriptive analytics or maybe they are and don't realize it. The reality is, just like all levels of analytics, there is a place for the democratization of prescriptive analytics throughout an organization but it may need to be viewed differently to how we think of the democratization of data in other levels of analytics. Herein is the need to democratize the results or the output of prescriptive analytics.

First, it may be confusing to think about democratizing prescriptive analytics for the first time. You may say to yourself, "but Jordan, come on now, the machines and technology are building out the output, how do you democratize that?" The reality is, we aren't democratizing the tools and technology, nor are we democratizing the skills needed to work within the technical side of prescriptive analytics (although, if you want to level up to that level of technical talent, please don't hesitate!). No, we are democratizing the output from the prescriptive analytics. This does require a certain amount of skill.

Now comes the world that my first book is about: data literacy. Please, everyone remember that you are already data literate. I think we do a disservice if we go around and tell people they aren't. Just because we have some level of data literacy doesn't mean that we have enough, though. We need to be confident and comfortable in using data and analytics in our careers, not just having the ability to use our weather apps. You have data literacy skills, but we all have areas where we can upskill and improve.

Data literacy is a necessary skill in an organization in order for the organization to be able to democratize prescriptive analytics. We need to have people with the ability to take the prescriptive analytics that are output from the machines and then understand them, apply them to the business goals and objectives that you, the team, or organization are trying to achieve. We need everyone to be able to take the prescriptive analytics and apply the human element to them. Remember, the machines have power, but so do we. We have the human element, the ability to successfully and intelligently bring our experience, thoughts, and abilities to the data. We need to do that.

Another element of democratizing prescriptive analytics is to get others involved in the process. If you are receiving output from prescriptive analytics, you are just one person. Now, people have busy jobs, but take the time to gather other thoughts and opinions around the prescriptive analytics. Then, we aren't sitting in our own tunnel of knowledge and thought, and we can gather different voices to the table.

Finally, another way to democratize prescriptive analytics, and it is a part of data literacy and data and analytics in general (and by the

way, I have spoken about it already): mindset. We need to democratize the right mindset throughout the organization when it comes to
prescriptive analytics. People fear what they don't know. People can
be intimidated and unsure with prescriptive analytics. If a machine is
just spitting out outputs and telling us what to do but a person doesn't
understand what is happening there or how it came to that solution,
do they trust it? Do they want to use it? I am not so sure. So, democratizing the right mindset is key to this. We will talk about the
democratization of mindset more in the next chapter.

Democratization of prescriptive analytics— tools and technology

Tools and technology are very important in the world of prescriptive
analytics. Now, this is an interesting topic because those who use the
tools to actually build prescriptive analytics are your more technical
and advanced data and analytics professionals. I hope that makes
sense by now. We will get to the tools and technologies that the end
users of the prescriptive analytics may use, but for now, let's look at
the tools used by the builders of prescriptive analytics.

From improvado.com we learn that Alteryx, RapidMiner, Birst,
and KNIME are among some of the tools for prescriptive analytics.[1]
Maybe you recognize these and maybe you don't. If not, that is ok,
you can always go and look them up. In short, tools should empower
those who are building prescriptive analytics to do so in a manner
that enables them to build powerful analytics that can be shared
throughout an organization. When shared throughout an organization, the results and the output, then prescriptive analytics are
democratized for the end user.

Another area of prescriptive analytics that we should be aware of
but isn't democratized in the same sense that business intelligence
tools may be is the world of coding. How many of you aren't those
who can code but want to learn how to become the most sophisti-
cated coding machine you have ever met? Did I hear crickets? Maybe?
In reality, you may be someone who wants to learn how to code, dive

in, become advanced, and then drive prescriptive analytics. That is awesome, I love it. For some of you, you may not want to do it at all! That is great too. Then there are those who are going to fall in the middle. Every single one of you, no matter where you fall on the spectrum I just listed, is fantastic and great. Remember, coding won't necessarily be passed around and democratized in the same way as tools. In fact, tools are coming along that can do that for you, like Seek AI. Seek AI is a tool that allows you to question the data and it will build the code for you. You can Google how to learn coding languages. With that, coding languages like SQL, Python, and R are great places to start.

Now, what about the end users—how are the tools and technologies democratized through prescriptive analytics? The short answer: they aren't. What is democratized or should be are the results and answers that roll through the tools and technologies. Then, the end user can make decisions on them. Now, does this mean that everyone in the company needs to know each and every prescriptive analytic that is produced? Of course not! Instead, it should be those who need to utilize the prescriptive analytic. Yes, you can share it throughout and that is what matters more. We need to give everyone the possibility of hearing. We need a culture that says yes, we can share these results. We need people who are comfortable questioning the results and combining the human element with them. Then you can make smarter data-driven decisions.

Data strategy

Prescriptive analytics is an interesting add within a data strategy. When does it come into place? Within Gartner's analytics maturity model it is last.[2] This model defines the maturity of analytics within an organization, with descriptive coming first all the way through to prescriptive at the end. Well, it should be. If you aren't doing descriptive analytics well, why would you progress? This is something I have spoken about. A lot of companies are stuck at descriptive analytics. Guess where they invest a lot of their money? In predictive and prescriptive analytics. The one that is forgotten is diagnostic analytics (the most important one, in my opinion). This is not how it should be done, no. Yes, we want to be able to utilize predictive and prescriptive analytics, for sure, but we need all four levels done holistically and that is a proper data strategy.

What I want from each organization is the proper investment into data and analytics. This includes the data strategy. Within the data strategy, we need to ensure that all four levels are accounted for PROPERLY! We need to be investing in all four levels, including prescriptive, but prescriptive should come later in the maturity of your organization, giving credit back to Gartner. Prescriptive analytics should be utilized and it should be a part of the strategy, but don't skip over steps to rush to the shiny object. Do things right!

Data storytelling

Now, here we have a great democratization of data throughout an organization through the proper communication of prescriptive analytics, and possibly combined with descriptive, diagnostic, and predictive. Data storytelling is so powerful. Prescriptive analytics is powerful, especially when combined with the human element. With this combination, we have the power to share it throughout an organization. Data storytelling should be utilized today across industries, powerfully and intelligently. When you have an analytic that is more technical, end users don't need to know the technical side. They need to know the analytic and they need to know the context. Across the data and analytics world, data storytelling should be utilized to harness the power of prescriptive analytics.

Industry examples

Here is a fun part of how prescriptive analytics can be utilized across the world. When we look at the examples we have used you can see how powerful it can be to have strong, quick computational analysis through prescriptive analytics. Think about the power of this during the Covid-19 pandemic. To have machines developing and driving modeling for the virus. Think of the power of machine learning and AI to help map and design vaccines. One thing we heard was that you can't design vaccines that fast and in traditional modeling, sure, but with the power of machine learning and AI, you can do things faster. Let's jump into our industry examples.

Healthcare

Within healthcare, the power of prescriptive analytics can be, well, powerful. Think about having an illness and having the ability to input your symptoms into the system. The machine learning or algorithm reads the data, computes through things, and then tells the doctor what you should do. This is power! Yes, some people may be fearful of this, but it is a tool for us. Combine the prescriptive analytics with the doctor to arrive at a good solution.

Let's now look at hospital beds. When we are computing the need for hospital beds and maybe looking at all the data with regard to a certain illness or something going around, think of how great it can be if the prescriptive analytic talks to us about what is happening and what we should be doing as a hospital.

Finally, think about Covid-19 and the pandemic. There was so much data going around. One, think about the vaccine and the power that can come from utilizing machine learning and modeling to arrive at medical interventions faster. Think about the power of prescriptive analytics to follow the data and find ways to combat or interact with the illness that caused devastation around the world. Think about utilizing prescriptive analytics not only for the treatment of patients with the virus itself but also for decision making for shutting down stores, looking at supply chain, and all the impacts the virus had around the world.

Within the healthcare field, the power of prescriptive analytics can help to enhance life. By inputting more and more data, allowing the machine learning to learn, we can utilize prescriptive analytics to improve health around the world.

Retail

I like the thought of prescriptive analytics in the retail space. Imagine if you are a clothing company, maybe like Old Navy or H&M, and you start to take data in and you are finding certain articles being purchased and certain articles not being purchased. You are taking in this data and combining it maybe with external data that can help shape both the clothing trends that are occurring but also taking in the economic trends themselves. This can help the clothing store to not only know what styles to sell and what ones to not sell, but it can also help the stores and companies to understand what economic conditions look like. We can then utilize prescriptive analytics to help us make these decisions.

Now, some people would say that we are just taking the human element out. No, no, no, I hope by now you understand how much I think the human element needs to be there. While the prescriptive analytics and data may be painting a picture, we need to combine that picture with the human element to make smart decisions for the companies themselves. Having only one or the other, the data or the human, is not the solution. We need to combine them together!

Going to our examples of stocking up and how many employees the store needs, I hope you can see how prescriptive analytics can help. As retail organizations are gathering the data, we can utilize prescriptive analytics to help us know how many items we need to stock. We don't want to get caught in a bad stocking situation. Second, with employees, utilizing prescriptive analytics, we can know how many staff we need at given time periods. This can help the employer not over- or under-staff and it can prevent the employee from being bored on the job.

Marketing

I hope this one goes without saying. In marketing I feel like we play an educated guessing game. We are reading the room, sort of, and we are making decisions on who to market to and why. Well, now let's bring in the power of prescriptive analytics to help us understand what to do. Utilizing the analytics appropriately and ethically—yes, I am using that word—we can see how we should be marketing and advertising to our current customer base and to prospective customers. We as humans only have so much ability and power to compute and do so much. Let's harness the power of prescriptive analytics to help us drive the solutions we need to be more effective in a marketing sense.

Finance, financial services, and banking

Prescriptive analytics can be a powerful tool for these types of organizations, but it must be done ethically (I will write on this below). For these types of organizations, having prescriptive analytics tell these companies what to offer, what to do with lending, what types of things to do, is powerful. Imagine having the computational power to make decisions as internal and external data is ingested throughout the organization. By having prescriptive analytics help to tell them what to do, these organizations can make smarter decisions.

Supply chain and logistics

Prescriptive analytics is a powerful tool these types of organizations should be utilizing. Machine learning, AI, and algorithms can be very helpful for these industries. Think of the Covid-19 pandemic when there were supply chain issues. With prescriptive analytics and modeling, the inputs could be coming in and it could have helped the situation. Now, I know that this was a different time, the pandemic, and not necessarily one that had been seen before. But the machine learning could have been, well, learning as the pandemic went on and hopefully provided help to supply chains and logistics. Within these fields there is the possibility of many moving parts. Having prescriptive analytics there to help can hopefully shore up the decision-making processes and help to overcome any obstacle.

Conclusion

Prescriptive analytics can be powerful in industries all over the world, but I will end this chapter with a caution or a short discussion of the ethical use of prescriptive analytics.

Data ethics and prescriptive analytics

Have you ever heard the term "black box" with regard to algorithms or data and analytics? This means an algorithm or something is operated but there is no transparency. Transparency in this case means we know the algorithm and how it works; we can see within it and understand how it is operating. Black box algorithm means we don't know; it is just that: a black box. We cannot just trust the machine learning, algorithm, or AI. We can't say, "well, the data said to do this." That is not going to cut it. This is one reason we need the intelligent combination of the human element with the data and technology. You can Google the unethical use of black box algorithms and other things. There is a book I would recommend by Cathy O'Neil called *Weapons of Math Destruction* if you are looking to understand potential destructive outcomes from prescriptive analytics.[3]

Overall, ensure data literacy in your organization and ensure you have a plan for the ethical use of prescriptive analytics.

Chapter summary

Prescriptive analytics is a powerful tool. As was mentioned before, this part of data and analytics comes later in your organization's data and analytics journey. Don't start investing in this right up front. Shore up your descriptive, diagnostic, and predictive analytics capabilities. Eventually, you can get to this part of your journey. But always remember the holistic approach to data and analytics. We want all four levels of analytics working to the benefit of an organization and to help it achieve its objectives.

> ### CHAPTER DEFINITIONS AND TAKEAWAYS
>
> - **Democratization of prescriptive analytics:** Like predictive analytics, prescriptive analytics is not democratized like descriptive or diagnostic analytics. Instead, the democratization comes in the sharing of the recommendations the machines have for us. The users then can combine their human element to make more intelligent decisions. This is key. We need to utilize these tools appropriately throughout an organization.
>
> - **Data ethics and prescriptive analytics:** Data ethics plays a big role within prescriptive analytics; it should be a part of all four levels, but especially with prescriptive analytics. We don't want to get caught up in a world where we just say the machine told us so and so we did it. No, we need to use our powerful human element to combine with data ethics so we use these tools and technologies more intelligently.

Notes

1 Friedman, H (2019) Top 10 prescriptive analytics tools, *Improvado*, https://improvado.io/blog/best-prescriptive-analytics-tools (archived at https://perma.cc/XKL3-JSZZ)

2 K, Taras (2016) 4 stages of data analytics maturity: challenging Gartner's model, LinkedIn, https://www.linkedin.com/pulse/4-stages-data-analytics-maturity-challenging-gartners-taras-kaduk/ (archived at https://perma.cc/6G3J-U6HF)

3 O'Neil, C (2017) *Weapons of Math Destruction: How big data increases inequality and threatens democracy*, Crown

15

How individuals and organizations can improve in prescriptive analytics

Let us turn to my analogy of doctors and getting sick. When we are sick, what do we sometimes get to help us out? A prescription. Let's think of this prescription as an external thing helping us to get better. That is how I want you to view prescriptive analytics. They are an external thing that is going to help us out. But, with prescriptions to help us feel better, sometimes we have to follow instructions. Maybe we have to take them with food. Maybe we are taking them at least twice a day. Maybe there is a descending pattern on how many you take a day. Whatever the case may be, you may have instructions to help you take them. Think of this the same as with prescriptive analytics. Maybe you have "instructions" or things that will empower you to take the prescriptive analytics. That's how I want to discuss improvement for individuals and organizations on prescriptive analytics. Please note that sometimes it is as easy as just taking a pill; sometimes the prescriptive analytics may be simple, but let's not count on that and improve as individuals and organizations to get better with this advanced analytic.

Data and analytic mindset and data literacy— prescriptive analytics

We spoke about this in the last section of analytics, predictive analytics, and the mindset is going to be similar, if not very close to the same. The reality is, when we think of how we can improve as individuals and organizations with prescriptive analytics, this can come down to the overall data literacy of the organization and the ability of the organization and individuals to drive decisions with the tools, technologies, and analytics that prescriptive analytics can drive. The reality is that the ability of the organization to drive prescriptive analytics does come down to data literacy; it can also come down to mindset.

Data literacy

How does data literacy play into the ability of an organization to utilize prescriptive analytics? The ability to read the results and the data from the prescriptive analytic, and then to utilize that to make a decision is crucial. The definition of data literacy from Qlik, and the one I used while working there and that I still use, is the ability to read, work with, analyze, and communicate with data. We need the prescriptive analytics to be utilized correctly. We need people to be able to read the data and information. We need them to work with it and in this case, the majority of people will just be utilizing the prescriptive analytic that has been presented to them. Instead, I want you to think of adding in your human element —don't just take what the machine gave you. Instead, combine your human element and the prescriptive analytic element. Finally, we need people to properly communicate the prescriptive analytic and how we are either taking it at face value or are shifting it some with the human element. Communication is the secret sauce of data and analytics, so with prescriptive and all levels of analytics, you need to be able to communicate it well. Let's chat about this communication briefly.

Communicate

If you are the one who is building the prescriptive analytics, your job is to be able to communicate it well to the masses so that they understand it. Don't communicate to your level of analytics. This is something that people need to understand with communication.

Knowing your audience is key! If your audience has the technical skills, then talk about the technical skills. If your audience doesn't have the technical skills, please don't communicate with technical jargon and wording. If you are receiving the prescriptive analytics, you can study and learn things. Take the time to think on the analytic or what is communicated with you. Take the time to learn key pieces. It isn't only on the technical people to communicate better with the masses. The masses should be working on their skills to understand better.

Mindset

Now, this isn't just about data literacy. Mindset is such a key thing for me. With prescriptive analytics, we need to have people understand the analytics maturity model from Gartner we have spoken about. We need to have a mindset that understands the data and analytics strategy. We need to understand each level of analytics, including prescriptive analytics. Herein we have mindset combining with data literacy. Remember, you already have data literacy but maybe you aren't fully data literate in all levels of analytics to the level you need to be. That's ok! Let's party! Never forget that. Instead, we have the analytics maturity model from Gartner. I want you to develop a similar analytics maturity mindset. This means you need to progress through the levels of analytics just like an organization progresses through them.

First, as you develop the skills within analytics, get good at descriptive analytics where you can read and understand what is happening. Make that a solid foundation. Your mindset should be to progress through the levels. Part of this mindset is to question the descriptive analytics. Then, we progress and have a mindset that says, "ok, I know what happened, let me ask a few questions to understand 'why'." This is your diagnostic analytics and having a mindset to question things and get to the why is what we want. Then, your mindset becomes one of knowing what happened and why it happened, at least having theories (finding a perfect why may be hard); we can move to the mindset that says, "alright, I am ready to predict stuff." We don't want to stop at the what and why, but we want to grow to what could be. This may be you building it or it may not. But we want to drive to predictions that can be built through predictive analytics and in some cases, prescriptive analytics. Our mindset needs to be, "this is a process and just because I have done all four levels of analytics doesn't mean we are done." I want you to know that it is an ongoing process. Sometimes, you may go from descriptive to diagnostic to descriptive. You may never use a prescriptive analytic. You may use the first three. But the mindset is one that knows this and is growing in data literacy so you can understand and read data better, one that can work with it better, one that analyzes it better, and one that communicates better. If you improve your data literacy skills, you can improve your skills with the four levels of analytics.

Prescriptive analytics and the tridata

Remember our wonderful tridata? Think about the elements: data-driven problem solving, data-driven decision making, and data-driven execution. How do you think prescriptive analytics can help the tridata? This is an inverse. We are not talking about how you can use these three things to improve in prescriptive analytics but instead how prescriptive analytics can help you with the tridata. I hope that makes sense. Let's jump in and discuss each level and the combination of the human element and the data. In this case, the prescriptive analytics.

Data-driven problem solving and prescriptive analytics

How many of you have nailed down your ability to problem-solve? Do you have it down to a science? You are probably better at it than you know. You are probably problem solving naturally each and every day. Maybe it is during a drive somewhere and you use GPS to help you get there. Maybe it is cleaning up in your house. Maybe it is in your job. But you are problem solving often. Now, what if we can enter a technology that will enable you to problem-solve even better? Now we are talking!

Within data and analytics, we are already seeing it in the augmentation of our analytics. The story of my trip to South Africa rings true here. While there, a gentleman asked me if the technology was going to make us lazy. I sure hope not! Technology is a tool to help us and enhance our work. Please don't get lazy because it is there helping do the jobs for us. Instead, I want you to use it to enhance your work. With the gentleman in South Africa I turned it on him. I said imagine you had a data and analytical task that would take you three hours. What if the technology can now do it for you in 15 minutes? That gives you two hours and 45 minutes to do the deep work, which is what Cal Newport speaks about in his book *Deep Work*.[1] Use the time to think on the problem. To think of what is happening. Now, use that with prescriptive analytics and data-driven problem solving.

Imagine you have a tool and technology that can help you paint a picture, provide you with analytics and data that can help you to solve problems. I sure hope you are taking advantage of it. Isn't it great that you have something that you can add to your tool belt to help you? That's how I want you to think about data and analytics and prescriptive analytics. What you are building is a skill set to be able to use the tools and data, and non-technical tools that may exist in data literacy, to enhance your abilities. Here, let's enhance our ability in data-driven problem solving. Can you see the beautiful work of the human and data elements coming together? I hope so!

Use the tools to help you think critically on the problem. Critical thinking is my third C of data literacy. In this case, you are looking at how the prescriptive analytic comes to you and you can think on it critically with a direct tie to the problem you are solving. When you receive the prescriptive analytic, I don't want you to sit there and say, "that can't be true." When we see data and analytics, I think this is something that unfortunately gets said a lot. Now, don't get me wrong, it could be false. That is not the point here. The reality is, I want everyone to have an open mind and open thoughts on the metrics and data placed in front of them. Instead of saying, "that can't be true" I want you to start asking, "could that be true?" With that question, you are using the mindset I want us to have. We are opening our thoughts to things.

With problem solving and prescriptive analytics, we don't want confirmation bias to creep in. Confirmation bias is looking for data to support our thoughts. So, when we are looking at prescriptive analytics, are we doing so with a lens that is hoping it supports our preconceived notions? I hope not. Instead, ask questions around it. If it does support what you are looking for ask yourself, "could this be false?" Then, investigate. If it doesn't support you and maybe completely goes against your thoughts, ask the question, "could this be true?" Then, investigate. Become the data-driven detectives for problem solving I know everyone can be.

Data-driven decision making and prescriptive analytics

Decision making is an interesting one. With prescriptive analytics, we may be inclined to think this is easy. The prescriptive analytic is telling us what to do. Well, it may be that simple, you are right. So, how do we get better as individuals and organizations with data-driven decision making and prescriptive analytics? The answer lies in the communication of the decision throughout.

We have spoken about mindset, we have spoken about questioning things and iteration, we have even spoken about communication, but now we want to talk about it specifically within decision making and I want to hit home on one key point: allowing people to share their thoughts on the decision.

Let me note first off that we don't live in a world, individually or organizationally, where we have all the time in the world to question things, right? I wish we did. I love to think. I love to ponder. I love philosophy. But in our world, sometimes decisions are quick and need to be made with cat-like reflexes. So, in this case there are two types of questioning I want you individually to improve on and organizations to add to their culture: post-decision questioning and pre-decision questioning. Let's look at the pre-decision questioning first.

Pre-decision questioning

When you do have time on decisions, say such as when you are doing a large product launch and looking to solicit ideas toward the product itself, you may be using prescriptive analytics to drive that decision. You may have actually used all four levels of analytics, but our chapter is on prescriptive. You are using prescriptive analytics and the data is showing that you lean in a certain direction with the product. As you do so, imagine you only take the prescriptive analytic and your solo interpretation—do you think you are providing enough backing to the decision? I would say no. If you have time, instead, what you want to do is create the culture for people to be able to come in and question things. This isn't just *allowing* it to occur but *inviting* it to occur. I want you to have such an open forum and discussion in your business that people are absolutely comfortable questioning the prescriptive analytics and the decision. "Why did the algorithm give this result?" Here is one that people may not like: "Can you tell me who is responsible for this machine learning decision? I just want to ask them a few questions." That one makes people defensive but it shouldn't. We need to have this open forum to question the prescriptive analytics and the decision. When we have enough time, allow questioning to occur throughout the organization with regard to the prescriptive analytics and the decision(s) it led to.

Post-decision questioning

Let me ask you this: Do you always have all the time in the world to make the decisions you want? Do you find yourself with such a "non-busy" life that you never, ever, have to make a decision with the snap of your fingers? Well, I am guessing no one is saying that and that is ok. Sometimes we don't have time to make the decisions in such a manner. That is ok. In business, it can be the same. Think of the Covid-19 pandemic. I know one company that wasn't ready to have everyone go remote; they weren't set up for that, so it took some time. I bet they would have loved to have more time or maybe not. Maybe it was the kick in the butt they needed.

The reality is, with our fast-paced world, decision making can be necessary in what seems like a split second. When you have your analytics rolling and things set up right, maybe you have your prescriptive analytics set up in a way that you can call upon it at any time. That would be wonderful, target for that. Then, when those split-second decisions come through, you can make them. What I want you to do is set up an environment where you question things after, hopefully, helping you to set up your business for better decisions in the future. The key is to not forget this type of questioning. You probably have a busy life, we probably all do. So, schedule time, however much it may be, to drive the questioning. Maybe you set up a meeting or a week each quarter that allows you to investigate the prescriptive analytics that were used to make a decision. Maybe you are just questioning the decision itself and all the levels of analytics that went into it. Just don't forget to make time for the questioning to occur. Hopefully, you gather more and more insight from it to help you make smarter decisions in the future.

Data-driven execution and prescriptive analytics

I am not sure a lot needs to be said here except to not get caught in analysis or perfection paralysis. It happens. It absolutely happens. We may think we are only part of the way there. We have used prescriptive analytics to help with problem solving and a decision, now we just have to implement and put that decision into place. That is fantastic! But wait, what if you did something different? What if we adjusted here or here or here? Did we get enough data? Did we have all the appropriate parties involved? Do we need to do something else? And on and on and on and on... Stop it! Yes, I love questions, I love them, but at times, if we are not moving forward because we won't stop asking questions, we are doing ourselves a disservice and possibly hindering our organization as a whole.

Instead, you can use the pre- and post-questioning I just mentioned above. You also just need to get comfortable with the iterative mindset. I hope we aren't seeking perfection. I want us seeking to be consistently good. Being consistently good will trump being occasionally perfect or great. So, get comfortable with not having all the answers and implementing the data-driven decisions. Then, iterate and roll with it.

Chapter summary

I cannot believe we are through all four levels of analytics at this point—this is exciting. I hope you have learned a thing or two throughout the chapters. In this chapter, we covered how individuals and organizations can improve in prescriptive analytics. If you are curious about things and see how you can implement them for you individually but are not seeing how you can do it organizationally, take a step back and think, if you are asking questions as an individual, maybe it then becomes fostering a culture in the organization of asking questions and allowing that safe space to do it.

In the next chapter, I will wrap all four levels of analytics into making a decision and give my tips and tricks for doing so. Let's jump in.

CHAPTER DEFINITIONS AND TAKEAWAYS

- **Prescriptive analytics and the tridata:** Prescriptive analytics can play a part within all three levels of the tridata, remember this. Harness the power of machines to help you problem-solve, make decisions, and if the machine can, to execute. If it isn't doing the execution, you are using the prescriptive analytics to help you come to a decision and then you are executing on that decision, so it does play a part in all three levels. I hope that makes sense for you.

Note

1 Newport, C (2016) *Deep Work*, https://www.calnewport.com/books/deep-work/ (archived at https://perma.cc/RH7G-ZKYP)

PART THREE

Bringing it all together

In the final two chapters, I hope I can bring together everything from the book. In Chapter 16, I will share my six-step program for individual and organizational analytical progression. Take notes, find where you fit within the six steps. One key thing I want you to do: question everything. Be curious and ask questions. Does this step apply to me? How can I apply this step to my current work, or can't I? Who do I know that is good at this step? Be curious and ask questions. Also, ask how you can be creative within the six steps.

The Conclusion will be a summary. I hope it has good reminders for you from the book and can help you drive understanding and knowledge. If you don't want to reread a whole chapter, don't—go to the end section of each chapter and then find the one that has the area you need. You can then go back into that chapter to learn more or reread it. Now, let's jump into Chapter 16.

16

Using all four levels of analytics to empower decision making

Six steps of analytical progression

OK, we have made it this far and we only have two chapters left, so what will we talk about? In this chapter, we are going to bring all four levels of analytics together to empower decision making. We have already talked about decision making, but this time we will be talking about a specific decision that will roll through the four levels of analytics. But wait, there is more to this chapter. I will be sharing with you my six-step program for individual and organization analytical progression. One thing I want you to gain from this six-step progression is that it isn't a one-size-fits-all solution. You personally will be somewhere along this progression program and that is wonderful. If you work in an organization, different areas of the organization will be at different stages of the progression. Some will be further along, some will be at the beginning, but know that you are working to get everyone up this mountain. Let me introduce you to the six steps:

1 Awareness
2 Understanding
3 Assessing
4 Questioning

5 Learning

6 Implementation

That's it, nothing fancy, no new or invented words, but it is a progression. To begin this chapter, let me walk you through each of the six steps; I will approach each step from two perspectives:

- if your organization is new or doesn't have a clue; and
- how to apply the step through the analytical process if you are on the journey already.

Then, we will use them in an example with the four levels of analytics. As I walk through that example, your job isn't to try to tie that *exact* example to your work but to use it for inspiration. When I have used personal and non-business examples in this book, I hope they are there to inspire you and help you recognize opportunities or examples in your life. OK, let's jump in.

Step 1: Awareness

At times when I speak I get asked, "How do I get a data literacy program going? How can I get those who haven't bought in to buy in and fully support a program?" This is a good question. Take a few moments to yourself and think, "How have I either been persuaded to buy into something or how do I think you can get people to buy into an idea?" One of the very first things you should be doing is bringing awareness to the organization of the idea or solution, and that is similar to the four levels of analytics.

What does awareness mean? To me, awareness is the knowledge of something. It is hearing or reading about an idea or something that is happening. Within data literacy, if I am building a program, I am going to want to have people aware of the idea, I am going to want to bring in speakers to help promote the idea. I want people to hear about it. Now, this partners closely with the second step, understanding, but we will get to that one shortly.

Awareness means to bring to the audience, whether individually or collectively as an organization, an idea, and having them listen to it.

I may do a public speaking session and speak for 35–45 minutes, bringing awareness to data literacy. That isn't true understanding but maybe they do get a little understanding; they may hear the "why" behind it, but that is step 1.

Within the four levels of analytics, we need an awareness of them. Did you know there were four levels of analytics before reading this book or hearing of this book? If not, hopefully I have brought awareness to you. I remember being at a dinner with an intelligent man who said people already knew about the four levels of analytics. No, they didn't. I am not sure why they didn't, but it may be because if you don't work in the world of data and analytics, you probably hear the term "analytics" alone. Sure, some may have heard of it and yes, some people knew of it, but not everyone. The first step is to bring awareness to the topic itself. With analytics, this is bringing awareness to each level, maybe sharing ideas or examples of descriptive, diagnostic, predictive, and/or prescriptive analytics. Bring awareness to your audience, whether great or small, to help drive the four levels of analytics success.

Another way awareness comes into play is if you are already an organization that is working with its data literacy and people are aware of the need for it, what about awareness around problems themselves? That is key. If an organization is running data and analytics, awareness becomes awareness of a problem or something we are trying to solve with data and analytics. Are we aware of the analytics being built? Are we aware of the four levels and how they are being used on a particular problem? Awareness is both about getting an organization going, and understanding problems, data, analytics, and what we are trying to solve. With awareness, we have a good starting point to progress through.

Step 2: Understanding

OK, hopefully by now in the book you have a good understanding of each of the four levels of analytics and contextually know what they are and how they work. Understanding is taking awareness to the next level. A business and personal example of this may help.

In business, you can't rely only on being aware of data and analytics or the tools to support them. You need to understand them. Now, this is done in context. Let's look at data visualizations. You may be aware of them, but to use them well you need to understand them and their purpose.

Within fitness, which plays such an important role in my life, both mentally and physically, being aware of such things as meditation, weightlifting, running, spinning, yoga, is good, but it isn't going to get us where we want to be. Instead of just being aware of something like meditation and knowing a little bit about it, I want us to understand what it is, how it works, and why it matters. That is understanding.

For example, we are aware that lifting weights is fantastic for our physical health, but do we truly understand how it plays a role in our fitness journey? We may be aware that meditation is powerful and great for us, maybe we have heard about it, but do we understand how it can help us with our mental health or to be mentally in a better spot? Here we see that progression from just being aware to understanding. We can take it to the next level.

That is the same with the four levels of analytics. We can be aware of each of the four levels, but with a true, solid understanding of each level, we have progressed beyond step 1 into step 2. Here, with a good understanding of each level, we can implement it better and more strongly. With a solid understanding of descriptive analytics, we are no longer just aware of data storytelling or data visualization, but we understand where it can fit into analytics or the business. With an understanding of diagnostic analytics and all four levels of analytics, we can understand that descriptive analytics is only the beginning, and in some cases all we need to build given context. But with a full understanding of the four levels of analytics, we have a good understanding of each level and its place in our journey.

Like awareness, there is another part of understanding, and all six steps in fact. There is an understanding of needing to take the organization forward with data literacy, but now let's look at it from individual and organizational perspectives if we understand about data literacy and data and analytics already. This understanding is about the problem itself and the analytics being used. We spoke about being aware of this and now you are progressing through analytics with an understanding of what is being done and why. You may follow this chain:

- You understand what descriptive analytics were used.
- You understand or have ideas around the why.
- You understand the predictive and prescriptive analytics.
- You have that understanding. You are progressing up the mountain.

Step 3: Assessing

OK, once we are individually aware of the four levels of analytics and understand them, what then? Well, we have to understand where we and/or our organization currently sit with our talents within the four levels of analytics. We can be excited, we can want to use all the levels, but without a solid understanding of our current skill level, we may not be ready to progress through the four levels of analytics. Instead, without an awareness, understanding, or assessment, we may be caught by the bright shiny object and purchase it, only to have it fall short. So, a solid step after the first two steps is to assess your personal skills and have an assessment for the whole organization. The whole organizational assessment can be a good map or compass to what you need to do. Why?

With an assessment of the whole organization, you are benchmarking where you stand at a current point in time. You know what your level is, but even better, by assessing an organization, you are opening up the door to understanding where there are strong skills and where there are not. This can help you to build out your support system for a data and analytics community, as it can inform people of where they are personally and where those with the needed skills reside. This can allow people to work with and find those who can help. A data and analytics community is something I am very big on for an organization's data-driven culture. By understanding who has what skills and where they sit in the organization you can roadmap out the plans of learning better and you can help drive evangelists or supporters of the data and analytics strategy you are implementing throughout the organization.

Here, this assessing is a part of a data literacy strategy. Data literacy should permeate throughout an organization. Data literacy is not a one-size-fits-all, nor does it take an hour-long workshop and you are there, boom, you have arrived at data literacy. You can work through the organization to upskill, but you need to know where to start with the knowledge base. You need to know where the skills gaps exist. You need to know who can do what and where. By assessing the organization and individuals, you can find where they are on the four levels of analytics spectrum and start to plug in the holes. Don't give them one workshop and think that's it. Instead, make it about prescriptive learning. Find the gaps and fill them in. You can even use prescriptive analytics to guide this; don't forget that you can use data to guide your learning journeys.

If you are an organization already on its journey, how does assessing come into play? Simply and straightforwardly, you need to assess what you are doing and progress into the next step, questioning. Think about that. You want to assess the four levels of analytics as this can help propel greater understanding. Assess each level— descriptive, diagnostic, predictive, and prescriptive. Gain a strong understanding of each utilizing the next step, questioning.

Step 4: Questioning

Curiosity is one of the most important aspects of data and analytical work. Questions spark the race. Questions spark the ideas. You then progress through the data and analytics journey. Without awareness, understanding, and assessing, you may not know how to question or even what you are questioning. In fact, you can say asking a question can come before any of the first three steps and fair enough. I want everyone to be more curious (one of my 3 C's of data literacy) and I want questions flying throughout an organization. In this case, though, I am talking about specific questioning within the four levels of analytics, so it's just a bit different. Here is what I mean.

With descriptive analytics, you can question:

- "Do we have enough data to help us gain a better understanding?"
- "Is there a better visualization we can use to drive the story of what is happening?"
- "This is a great descriptive analytic, but what does it mean? Why does the visualization look the way it does? What is the trend and why is it happening?"

See, I have jumped into diagnostic analytics or propelled us into it. You have the descriptive analytic and you start to turn the what into a why. That is diagnostic analytics. Ask questions like:

- "Why are we seeing this?"
- "Why did you use that visualization to do this—can we improve on it because I am not seeing or able to find the why here?"
- "Why do we even care about this data, what is the point?"

The progression continues. Now, we know a why and we start to question:

- "What does this mean for the future?"
- "How can we use this to help predict models?"

Then, we are building predictions and we can question those predictions. Finally, we have the power of the machine and we start to utilize the machine learning we have to help us build out prescriptive analytics. Then, we can question:

- "How does the human element fall into place with this prescriptive analytic?"
- "How can I bring my thoughts and gut feel to this prescriptive analytic?"

See, questioning things. This is power as it can move the analytical journey forward in a powerful way. Become aware, understand, and assess. Then, build your skills and get really good at asking questions.

As we are speaking about each step in two different contexts, one where individuals or organizations are new to this and one where they are not, the questions above help in either case.

Step 5: Learning

Now that we have our questions rolling, and there is probably an infinite number of possibilities of questions for all realms of analytical possibility, we then jump into our learning and progress through our four levels of analytics.

The questions we ask may spark us to learn what is happening and then we seek and find new ways of doing things within the four levels of analytics. With descriptive analytics you may ask why you used a certain visualization; you can learn the answer to why it was chosen, then come up with new ideas for a new visualization you could use to drive home more understanding or improve upon it to help you with diagnostic analytics. Then, when you are seeking to understand the why, maybe you are learning new things. This could march you down the same path you have been going or it may march you down a different path, and that is ok. This is you learning and progressing. With your learnings, you can build predictions and then assess how well those predictions have gone. You are learning, modifying, and growing. Finally, you can learn what the prescriptive analytic says and combine it with the human element, only to not believe the prescriptive analytic is right or feel you need to go a different direction. Wonderful—learn and progress.

As we look at this through two lenses, beginners and those already moving, learning can have two facets. One, learning from a data literacy perspective to gain knowledge on how to do things better and two, learning around the four levels of analytics and how they address a problem. Then, making smarter, more informed decisions about things, and driving it to the next level: implementation.

Step 6: Implementation

Now, with all this learning and growth through the analytical progression, you are now needing to implement. You can't sit back and think on the data and answers you have developed—you need to execute. You need to make decisions and you need to execute on the ideas. An idea within data and analytics is wasted without execution of some kind, even if that is just thinking about the idea. Utilize your progression here and drive the execution of ideas and strategies.

Making a decision with the four levels of analytics

Now, let's use these six steps to drive us to a decision, combining with the four levels of analytics. Now, I am not going to use all six steps with all four levels of analytics; that may cause a very long chapter. Instead, I will hopefully spark some ideas on how to use them and hopefully help you to use the six steps and four levels appropriately. I am going to choose to write about a personal example and then a business example: preparing for another ultra-marathon and building a marketing campaign. My hope is that whether I use a personal or a business example, what I want this to do is spark an idea in your mind of what you can do, whether personal or business. We are not going to have the same concerns, problems, or ideas in our personal lives or business lives, and if we do, more power to us. But I feel a personal example can feel, well, more personal. Let it inspire you in your personal life. A business example can help inspire you at work, and both types can help inspire you in different ways. Just having a hypothetical business example might not spark enthusiasm within you or drive anything. Instead, let's make the personal example about a struggle I had and then spark ideas and discussion within yourself on your own personal journey with the four levels of analytics.

Personal example

To prepare for an ultra-marathon takes time and dedication, and the use of data is powerful. My journey with Speedgoat last year was not what it could have been. I was running it solo, I had my trekking poles, I had the benefit of having run it twice before, but nothing prepared me mentally for what I experienced. It was painful, not enjoyable, and I am not sure I have ever wanted to quit a race more in my life. But I made it through with a big help from my family coming to one of the peaks. Without them showing up, I'm not sure I would have finished. I had a desire to miss a cutoff, but never did, so I kept going. How can I use my six-step progression to help me improve? How can I combine it with the four levels of analytics? And the absolutely most important question here: how can you use the six steps and the four levels within your personal life and your career? How can an organization do this? Remember, these six steps and four levels can be utilized to help with building new or enhancing existing products, for hiring processes, for marketing campaigns, for personal goals. Use them!

To begin, while writing this book I was invited to run a 50-mile ultra-marathon. To start, I need to build descriptive analytics for myself around race prep and what I need to do. I need to use my six-step process and develop an awareness and understanding of my current state of fitness. What do I weigh? Is that too much to carry for a 50-mile race? Where is my cardio fitness at right now? How is my flexibility? What is my nutrition like? How is my hydration (oh, the killer of the Speedgoat 50k race this year)? To begin, I can start to build out descriptive analytics to know my state of being. This can help me to drive awareness and understanding, which had better propel me to different and better work to get me ready (if I were to race, from the time of writing, I have about seven and a half months to get ready—more than enough time with my background and experience).

So, we are seeing awareness and understanding already, and in fact, I didn't mention it, but we are assessing too. We can use both descriptive and diagnostic analytics to do this. We can drive home an understanding of what is happening, where I currently am with my fitness level, and I can understand why it is happening.

Using both descriptive and diagnostic analytics, I can also now drive home my questioning and learning. "OK, last year, I was not where I needed to be for the Speedgoat 50k, that is definitely apparent, but I need to know why that was." So, I can ask questions. I have ideas. I don't think my mental health was where it needed to be, dragging down my energy and physical workouts. My physical fitness wasn't where it should have been, so I need to do better in my training, both mental and physical, this year.

With this understanding, I can now use my learnings to build new plans. I can utilize the sixth step of implementation with predictive and prescriptive analytics. I can build some training goals and predictions for each month leading to the race. I can use "prescriptive analytics" which may not be from a machine but from an external source, like my wife helping me stay on top of my training or an online training plan that has been built with knowledge and expertise. Now, this isn't a machine learning plan, which maybe I can use to build training for me—that would be fun—but I can use external things to help me drive my plan.

From all of this work, I can prepare and train for the race, iterating as I go, and hopefully progress through a plan that will enable me to be successful.

Business example

For our business example, let's look at building a marketing campaign. To begin with, steps 1 and 2, awareness and understanding, can be built with descriptive analytics. You can utilize descriptive analytics to understand demographics, spending patterns, or how other campaigns have performed. You are gathering your awareness and understanding of what is happening.

Once you have your awareness and understanding, you can dig in and find some diagnostic analytics. This is especially true if you are looking at previous marketing campaigns. How can diagnostic analytics help here? If you are understanding "why" things are happening with descriptive analytics, you should be able to build out better marketing campaigns. How can you get good at diagnostic analytics? You should use steps 4 and 5. By questioning and learning, you are figuring out why things are occurring.

With knowing the "what" and the "why" through descriptive and diagnostic analytics, we can move towards predictive analytics. We want to build out the predictions for the campaign. We can also utilize prescriptive analytics, if we have the technology bringing it to us.

Finally, after all of this has been done, we need to follow step 6: implementation. Just put the campaign to work. You can do it. Then, utilizing your skills, you assess it and understand how the campaign has done and iterate. You can do this!

Chapter summary

But, this isn't just about racing, this is about you! What can YOU do to use the six steps and four levels of analytics to drive better decisions in your life? What can YOU do to use the six steps and four levels of analytics to make better decisions in your job? This isn't just about YOU, though. This is about organizations, too. What can organizations do to utilize the six steps and four levels of analytics?

Some may think of this as a business book and not like the personal examples, and that is absolutely wonderful. I tie in personal examples and love to. Personal examples make things more real, like thinking about the doctor and the four levels of analytics, or me and my racing. What I hope those examples will do is spark something within you to drive analytics yourself. What I encourage you to do is write it all down and journal. As ideas come to you, write them and then dissect them through analytics. What a wonderful thing that can be! Use this book as your guide to drive better analytical work.

I cannot believe we are here. I hope you have enjoyed this book. I don't want you to memorize it all, no. I hope that it has sparked some curiosity and a desire for you to enhance your abilities in the four levels of analytics. Use this book along with my two other books, *Be Data Literate* and *Be Data Driven*, to enhance your data and analytical journey. I didn't write them from a purely technical angle. I didn't write them to teach you statistics or coding. There are plenty of books out there like that. I hope they spark your journey! Now, let's conclude with a summary chapter.

CHAPTER DEFINITIONS AND TAKEAWAYS

- **My six-step analytical progression:** These are six steps to analytical work. Now, you may be at one level and others at a different level and that is ok. The six steps are:

  o Awareness

  o Understanding

  o Assessing

  o Questioning

  o Learning

  o Implementation

- **Awareness:** You are aware of the data and analytics, but are new and not too sure. That's ok, you are in the beginning phase and can progress.

- **Understanding:** You now have progressed beyond awareness and you understand the four levels of analytics, but you are still in the early stages. You may have some understanding but that doesn't mean you are comfortable working within the four levels of analytics.

- **Assessing:** This is twofold. One, with data literacy, we are assessing our skill level or the skill level of the organization and that is great. Two, we are assessing where we are in the analytical journey. We are assessing things, and this leads to questioning, the next step.

- **Questioning:** We need to get good at asking questions, so do it. Don't be afraid to ask! Kids are wonderful examples of asking questions. They just do it and we can too, so get asking.

- **Learning:** There are also two sides to this coin. One, we are learning to improve in our data literacy and two, we are learning what is happening and learning along the four levels of analytics.

- **Implementation:** We are implementing our new learning, whether it is us who is learning. What learning do we need to do to improve in our skills within the four levels of analytics? Also, we are implementing our learnings within the four levels of analytics.

Conclusion

To conclude, let's make your life easier. For your benefit, I am going to create a summarized version of the book. This way, you can turn to this chapter for a refresher instead of reading the whole thing again. You don't always need to reread a whole book to refresh on something. If you do decide to reread it, great. I hope each time that you do so, you learn something new. Don't forget to take notes each and every time (journaling is a big thing for me). I won't just write summaries of the chapters; you can go back and review the book however you want. Instead, I will break it down by sections or topics. Hopefully, this will be a refresher and a takeaway for you. Then, you can go back to chapters or areas of the book that talk about these topics and drive them home for yourself. I hope you enjoy your nerdy journey because nerds are amazing and awesome. You should be proud to be one.

Going to the doctor

To begin, let's turn back to the example of the doctor to help refresh our minds on the four levels of analytics and how they work. Remember, you are sick. What is the process a doctor may go through to help you get better? They may describe your sickness or you may describe your symptoms (descriptive analytics). Then, the doctor "diagnoses" you (diagnostic analytics). With an understanding of "why" you are sick, the doctor can make predictions of how to get better (predictive analytics). Then, the doctor may prescribe medicine to you (prescriptive analytics). Now, remember, doctors don't always get it right and neither does data and analytics. Instead, we need an iterative mindset to succeed.

Iterative mindset

What exactly is an iterative mindset? An iterative mindset knows that data and analytics isn't perfect, it isn't the pot of gold at the end of the rainbow. Data and analytics should guide us on the journey to that pot of gold. What we need to do is understand that the data and analytics won't always get it right, the predictive analytics may be totally off. That is ok. Instead, we learn from it and continue on the journey of the four levels of analytics over and over and over again. Fail often and learn from it, keep the journey rolling.

The tridata

The tridata consists of three elements: data-driven problem solving, data-driven decision making, and data-driven execution. Remember, we don't chase the bright, shiny object. Instead, we utilize data and analytics to help us achieve business outcomes and goals. That's what we should be using them for—they are tools. So, utilize descriptive, diagnostic, predictive, and prescriptive analytics to drive us toward or help us in problem solving, decision making, and execution. Remember, we can't forget to execute on things.

The four levels of analytics—one by one

Descriptive analytics

Descriptive analytics is the "what" of analytics. What is happening, what may be happening—it is a description of things. For me, I can look at my Speedgoat race and find an analytic telling me I lost over 23 pounds of sweat in the race. That is a descriptive analytic. I can utilize that to help me and propel me toward understanding why I struggled so much in the race.

A descriptive analytic is delinquency and write-off rates. A descriptive analytic is how well a marketing campaign did. Remember, a descriptive analytic is not a "why" but a "what." The second level is the "why" level.

Diagnostic analytics

Diagnostic analytics is the most important level of analytics, in my opinion. The reality is we can understand what is going on and that is great, but if we don't understand why it is happening then how can we build out strong predictions? How can we make better data-driven decisions? We have to be intelligent in this aspect. We need to know the "why." Utilize diagnostic analytics to determine ideas around the why. Now, don't get caught in analysis or perfection paralysis, no. Instead, we need to have ideas about "why" things occurred and remember that correlation doesn't necessarily mean causation. Instead, we can be smart about things, drive answers, iterate, and continue on in our progression.

Predictive analytics

The third level of analytics and one which should be built after we know why things are occurring is predictive analytics. We build predictions to see what could happen. With a good understanding of what happened (descriptive analytics) and why it happened (diagnostic analytics), we are positioned to build predictions to help us understand the possible future. Then what do we do? We iterate and drive forward. We build new descriptive analytics after we analyze the prediction, we understand why it occurred after the prediction, and then we build new predictions. Here is the holistic approach to data and analytics.

Prescriptive analytics

OK, let's move over to let the machines take over. No, no, no, the human element absolutely has a crucial place at the data and analytics table. All of you, yes, all of you and all of those you work with, have a place at the data and analytics table. The prescriptive analytic is another tool in our tool belt for success. We allow the machines to learn and to give us analytics, telling us what to do. That is ok—we then can iterate and move on, we can drive forward using all four levels to make decisions.

The purpose of data and analytics

What is the purpose of data and analytics? It is to help us make better decisions and to achieve our personal goals, or to help organizations achieve their goals. There you go, end of story. Don't be intimidated by data and analytics; utilize or enhance your data literacy and use these things as empowering tools in your life. If you are a part of an organization, utilize data and analytics to achieve their goals. If you are an organization, do this right. Don't buy the bright, shiny object. Instead, invest properly, hire the right people, have the right culture, and do this the correct way, eliminating data and analytical debt. Doing this the right way can pay immense dividends!

Bringing it all together in your business
and personal life—key takeaways

As we end the book, let me provide you with a list of key takeaways that can empower you in your personal life. I hope that you have enjoyed it, but it isn't just about enjoying the book—I want you to walk away with a few things you can do. Here is a list:

- Why do I share examples with you? Well, one key thing I want you to take away from the examples, whether personal or in your business life, is ideas. Ideas around what you can do. Ask yourself,

"Do I have examples in my own life like this and can I apply the four levels of analytics to those examples?"

- Think analytically. One thing I want you to do in your life is to think more analytically. What in the world do I mean here? I want you questioning things. Question things and walk around and dive deeper into them. Does this mean you need to do advanced analytics on things? No, of course not. But it could mean you find the "what" and the "why" more.

- Mindset. I have spoken a lot on mindset. I want you to have the right, iterative mindset in your life. Sometimes things won't go the way you like, but does that make it bad? No! Just like our doctor who diagnoses disease and illness isn't going to always get it right, neither will you in your life. Learn and grow within it. Use the opportunity to learn more "whats" and more "whys."

- Tools and technologies. Now, are data literacy and analytics all about tools and technologies? No, they aren't! But tools and technologies are powerful in your life and they are in data and analytics. So, go out and see if you can develop some skills in tools and technologies.

Now, I bet you have examples, tools, technologies, and things in your life that you didn't even know could apply to data and analytics. You do! Don't underestimate your skills and abilities. Are you data literate? Of course you are! Can you do analytics? Yes, everyone can! From a wonderful book by Category Pirates called *Snow Leopard*, a key takeaway I have is that you want to write a book toward the person, helping them to understand how it applies to them, how they can grow from it.[1] Well, I hope you have found ways you can personally develop and grow from this book. Each one of you has a seat at the data and analytics table. Are you ready to feast? Let's do this!

Note

1 Category Pirates (2022) *Snow Leopard: How legendary writers create a category of one*, https://www.categorypirates.com/store/snow-leopard-how-legendary-writers-create-a-category-of-one (archived at https://perma.cc/UB4N-Z62H)

INDEX

The index is filed in alphabetical, word-by-word order. Numbers are filed as spelt out; acronyms and abbreviations are filed as presented. Page locators in italics denote information within a figure.

CPSIA information can be obtained
at www.ICGtesting.com
Printed in the USA
JSHW041913220523
42081JS00004B/12